Knickers in a Twist

Knickers in a Twist

A DICTIONARY OF BRITISH SLANG

JONATHAN BERNSTEIN

CANONGATE

Edinburgh · New York · Melbourne

First published in Great Britain in 2006 by
Canongate Books Ltd., Edinburgh, Scotland

Printed in the United States of America
ISBN 978-1-84195-834-7
eISBN 978-1-5558-4794-4

Canongate Books Ltd.
an imprint of Grove Atlantic
154 West 14th Street
New York, NY 10011

Distributed by Publishers Group West

groveatlantic.com

21 22   18 17

To my family

Contents

Special thanks to Jim Greer and Julius Bernstein

Introduction

If you like plonk, are you a plonker? If you have a minge, does that make you a minger? If you are a slag, does that mean you should be slagged? If you've got bottle, is there a chance that you might bottle it? If you're a slapper, does that automatically make you a happy slapper?

As a Los Angeles–based, green card–carrying Scot who returns with reasonable frequency to his native land, I'm in a pretty good position to comment on the similarity between the United States and the UK. Walking the mean streets of Glasgow, I see a Gap, a Subway, a McDonald's, an Arby's, a Borders, a Burger King, a Starbucks, and a Blockbuster. Online, I order goods from Amazon.com. On TV I can, if I wish, watch *Lost, Desperate Housewives,* ballroom-dancing D-list celebrities, and Simon Cowell crushing the dreams of deluded crooners. Hollywood's fear of piracy has made the international release date more frequent with the result that the lineup of entertainment at the British multiplex is similar to that on offer in any American mall. America's presence both in the mercantile and in the social lives of the British is pervasive enough to inspire dark thoughts of cultural imperialism.

Then the British open their mouths and all such thoughts vanish. It's not just the accents that render non-posh Brits all but incomprehensible to the majority of Americans. It's the euphemisms, the abbreviations, the colloquialisms; it's the slang. American sitcom writers looking to amuse themselves have made a practice of slipping the epithet "wanker" into otherwise innocent chunks of dialogue. Mike Myers successfully propelled "shag" into the U.S. lexicon. But beyond that lies a vast and teeming morass of head-scratchers. What's an ASBO? Or a bovver boy? A chav? A bell-end? What's the difference between a bap and baps?

The aim of these unscholarly pages is to guide you through the jungle of British slang, uncovering the etymology but also illuminating the correct usage. After all, British slang is largely class-based. You have to be aware of how to utilize it with the appropriate degree of condescension, belligerence, or glee. In the following pages, the mysteries of cockney rhyming slang, of Polari (the secret gay code of the 1950s and '60s), of TV catchphrases, of the criminal classes, of the sports field, and of the bedroom will be dispelled in order to bring about greater communication and understanding between our two great nations. And if it doesn't accomplish that at least you'll be aware that when a British citizen describes you as a wally, a herbert, a spanner, or a bampot, he is not showering you with compliments.

Oh yes, and the answers to the opening questions are: sometimes, not necessarily, only in extreme circumstances, no, and I hope not.

Jonathan Bernstein
Los Angeles, January 2006

Acronyms

ASBO

Anti-Social Behavior Order. Introduced in 1998 to put the fear of God and possible incarceration into drug dealers, joyriders, underage smokers and drinkers, beggars, drunks, graffiti artists, litter louts, and those unable to modify the volume of their profanities. If you are guilty of one of the aforementioned infractions, you are eligible to be slapped with an ASBO, which has the effect of banning you from the area in which you perpetrated your devious behavior and also "naming and shaming" you by plastering a picture of your scowling mug across local papers and fly posters. If you breach the terms of your ASBO, whether by venturing back into the area where you offended or resuming your frowned-upon activities, you lay yourself open to a prison term of up to five years. More than 6,497 ASBOs had been issued by June of 2005, and not just to fractious adolescents as the 2006 UK TV documentary *OAPs on ASBOs* was only too happy to illustrate.

BSE

Bovine spongiform encephalopathy or, as it's more widely known, mad cow disease

C of E

Church of England, notably founded by Henry VIII in response to the pope's refusal to grant him a divorce from one of his several wives

CV (curriculum vitae)
Résumé, list of lies

GBH
Grievous bodily harm: very serious injury suffered by the victim of a crime (see also **GBH of the earhole**)

GBP
Great British Pounds

GCHQ
Government Communications Headquarters; labyrinthine intelligence and security organization that lets Britain sleep soundly without questioning the methods used to maintain our continued peace of mind because *we can't handle the truth!*

GCSE
General Certificate of Secondary Education. American equivalent: SATs.

GP (general practitioner)
Doctor. American equivalent: butcher.

HMRC
Her Majesty's Revenue and Customs: the government department responsible for collecting VAT revenue, customs duties, and preventing drugs, alcohol, and tobacco being smuggled through customs. I've been sneaking haggis in and out for years. Never been caught.

HMS
Her Majesty's Ship

M & S
Long-surviving department store chain Marks & Spencer (also known, affectionately, as Marks & Sparks), renowned for its comfortable undergarments and tasty prepacked meals

MOD
Ministry of Defence

MOT
The Ministry of Transport's mandatory yearly test of a vehicle's roadworthiness; if the ropey old banger passes the test, the driver gets to display a certificate on the inside of the windscreen.

OAP (old age pensioner)
Senior citizen

OHMS
On Her Majesty's Service

PMQ
Prime Minister's Question time: the PM answers—or evades—questions from members of parliament in the House of Commons every Wednesday from 12:00 to 12:30.

QUANGO
Quasi Non-Governmental Organization: autonomous local government department with hazily defined function. Generally, they have titles that suggest they have something to do with housing or transport or health but, in fact, their main function is to perpetuate bureaucracy. The cynical may suggest that these committees and agencies exist solely to reward close but otherwise unemployable associates of the political party in power.

TA
Territorial Army. U.S. equivalent: National Guard.

VAT
Value added tax; similar to sales tax, except much, much more rapacious

WC
Water closet (toilet). American equivalent: restroom, bathroom.

Bad Behavior
"Ready to Ruck!"

Aggro
Aggravation; also, more uncommonly, aggression (also, **bovver, bovver boys, bovver boots**)

Beer monster
Heavy drinker prone to loutish behavior (also **lager lout**)

Bovver
Cockney pronoun meaning bother; activity practiced by trouble-loving hooligans prevalent in late 1960s/early '70s known as bovver boys.

Bunk off
Play hooky

Casuals
Football supporters who came to prominence in the late 1970s, standing apart from the thuggish morass by wearing expensive European designer clothes that they'd picked up on trips following their favorite clubs abroad.

Chav
Much-mocked and maligned British working-class youth dressed in Burberry, hoop earrings, thick neck chains, and white sneakers. The slang word "chav" was used in Chatham during the early 1990s (and possibly earlier), as well as the word "Pikey," to refer to someone who was or had a traveler appearance. The

meaning has changed over the past ten to fifteen years, especially since it has been picked up by the media. "Chav" is no longer synonymous with "Pikey," and describes a separate subculture. "Chav" is commonly thought to derive from the mid-nineteenth-century Romany word "chavi." It is sometimes mockingly redefined as an acronym for Council Housed and Violent, Council Housed and Vile, Council House Assault and Violence, Council House Associated Vermin, Council House Adolescent Violence, and Council House Adidas Victim. While *Little Britain*'s Vicky Pollard and *The Catherine Tate Show*'s Lauren instantly became nationally beloved sketch-show chav caricatures, these fictional representations are smaller than life. This is borne out by Britain's endless fascination with the generously cantilevered, tandoori-tanned glamourpuss Jordan who reigns as first lady of the chavs. The sound track to the chav lifestyle is provided by Mike Skinner, who records successfully under the moniker the Streets, and the pint-sized female rapper Lady Sovereign, whose

Chavette
© Josephine Soughan & Simon Pentleton/PYMCA

U.S. signing to Def Jam is a clear indication that label president Jay-Z is having a laugh.

Chiseler
Cheat, crook, con man

Do a runner
Exit a restaurant or place of business without paying (common practice among chavs).

Ducking and diving

Term used to describe the manner of answer given when the target of the inquiry doesn't want anyone to know what manner of deviant behavior hc's actually involved in. Probable derivation from boxing, in which case its American equivalent would be "bobbing and weaving."

Flit

Sneak out of rented accommodation without informing the landlord or paying the rent

Happy slapping

Crazy prank where psycho kids slap innocent victims across the face and capture the results on their mobile phones

Laddette

Young female with a bottomless appetite for drinking, vomiting, casual sex, fighting

Lager lout

Young man with a bottomless appetite for drinking, vomiting, casual sex, fighting, taunting moggies

Ned

Violent working-class youth (chiefly Scottish), said to be an acronym for Non-Educated Delinquent

Play truant

Play hooky

Pull a sickie

Pretend to be unwell in order to absent yourself from work.

Seagulling

The success of *Harry Potter* has led to a universal impression that all British children are as charming and resilient and downright decent as Harry, Hermione, and Ron. That impression is not erroneous. The little Brits are adorable with their accents, their ruddy cheeks, their bright sparkling eyes, and their quaint little habits, such as seagulling. First spotted in January of 2006 as an amusing bit of mischief worth noting. Seagulling involves one school chum having a good time with himself and subsequently slapping the sticky residue across the unsuspecting face of the first victim to wander into his vicinity. Like I said, *adorable!*

Terrace anthem

Fight song performed with great gusto by soccer fans—the hooligan and the supporter alike—with the intention of intimidating the opposition. Every club has its own anthem but they can pretty much all be summed up by the sentiments of the ultimate anthem: "You're Gonna Get Your Fuckin' Head Kicked In!"

Under the cosh

Under the threat of imminent violence. U.S. equivalent: under the gun.

Wangle

Devious scheme

"I wangled my way into the club without paying. Good for me!"

Wind up

Lie to or trick someone for the purposes of gaining amusement from their frustration (also **wind up merchant**)

"I told him he'd won half a million nicker on the lottery. He ran out and bought a house for his mum, then I told him I was just winding him up. Should have seen his face."

Wobbly

Untrustworthy

Yob

A lout or hooligan, boy spelt backward (also **yobbo**)

Body Language
"Has Anyone Seen My Little Willy?"

Auxters (sometimes spelled Oxters)
Armpits (chiefly Scottish/Irish)

Baps
Breasts

Bell end
Dick head (literal sense)

Bingo wings
Unsightly blobs of loose skin hanging from the unexercised upper arms

Bonce
Head

Boss-eyed
Cross-eyed

Brewer's droop
Inability to achieve erection after imbibing too many pints of beer down the old boozer with your stupid mates

Bumfluff
Wispy strands of facial hair foolishly sported as beard and mustache substitutes. U.S. equivalent: peach fuzz.

Dangly bits
Male genitals

Family jewels
Male genitals. (It could also mean a collection of gems that have been passed down from generation to generation, accruing in sentimental and actual value. But it's generally understood to refer to the cock and balls.)

Fanny
Vagina. Of particular note to Americans when traveling in the UK: *Do not* under any circumstances utter the otherwise harmless phrase "My fanny hurts from sitting on the Tube all day" in either polite or impolite company, especially if you are male. And UK tourists in the States should not expect anyone to take offense when shouting "My fanny!" in public. Also, when an American casually refers to his or her "fanny pack," please refrain from falling over laughing.

Goolies
Testicles

Goose pimples
Goose bumps

Hooter
Nose (also **conk**)

John Thomas
Penis

Lady-bazzers
Breasts

Laughing gear
Mouth

Lug-holes
Ears

Mush
Mouth

Old chap
Penis

Percy
Penis (Possibly inspired by the 1971 film of the same name involving a penis transplant.)

Phizog
Face (from "physiognomy")

Sauce-shelf
Breasts

She's got the decorators in
She's on her period (also **she's got the painters in**)

Shell-like
Ear

Tadger
Penis

Tradesman's entrance
Anus

The trouser department
The male genitals

"He's a bit lacking in the trouser department."

Wally dugs
False teeth (chiefly Scottish)

Willy
Penis (also **winkle**)

Catchphrases
"They Don't Like It Up 'em!"

Oi, Madonna! Swill all the Guinness you can stomach. Dress yourself in Barbour jackets and flat caps. Converse in the cut-glass tones of a Windsor. You may not sport a fanny pack and a camcorder but you're no better than a tourist. You betrayed an amazing lack of grasp of the British character with your smug revelation that you refused to allow your children to watch television and that you yourself are unsullied by exposure to the evils of the flat screen. Raise your children however you see fit, but that anti-TV stance was pretty much an admission that when she moves outside her tight circle of minions, lackeys, and supplicants, Madonna *has no idea what anyone in Britain is talking about!* That's because everyone in the UK converses, at least in part, in catchphrases derived from ancient and current sitcoms and game shows. Now you, like Madonna, may protest that paying attention to catchphrases from idiotic TV shows you've never seen and never will see is a waste of a few moments of your life you could devote to co-opting obscure aspects of underground culture and leeching them of all originality. Let me rebut with the suggestion that you will, at some point, converse with a Brit. Whether a toff or a commoner, they will throw what seems like a bizarre non sequitur into the conversation. They're not being willfully obscure; they're conversing in catchphrase and, unless you want to go through your UK experience wearing a permanent blank look (like Madonna), you would be well advised to familiarize yourself with a few of these evergreens.

"I'm a lady"; "I am the only gay in the village."

The actor/writers behind the phenomenally successful sketch show *Little Britain* may have received more praise for any given minute of their series than Dick Emery did during his entire career but in their enthusiasm for portraying grotesque female characters and beating a catchphrase to death, they are his spiritual descendants.

"Just like that. Not like that. Like that."

Catchphrase of perhaps the most beloved of British comedians, the comedy magician Tommy Cooper. It's a measure of the high esteem in which Cooper continues to be held that his gags and catchphrases remain in the national memory almost thirty years after he died live on TV in the middle of his act.

"My pussy . . ."

The highlight, if that's the correct term, of every episode of the shriekingly broad department store sitcom *Are You Being Served?* arrived when saleswoman Mrs. Slocombe responded to a mundane morsel of information with a sentence that started with the words "My pussy . . .", i.e., "I hope they keep the noise down tonight," "Oh, me too. My pussy was climbing the walls last night." I'm laughing just thinking about it.

"Nice to see you. To see you . . . nice!"

Bruce Forsyth, now nearing eighty, has been the UK's leading light entertainer for almost fifty years (he currently hosts *Strictly Come Dancing,* the original British version of *Dancing With the Stars*); newborn babies and husks of humanity clinging to life enjoy equal familiarity with his immortal catchphrase (which requires audience participation on the climactic "Nice!").

"Ooh you are awful . . . but I like you."

Camp British comic Dick Emery had a sketch show that ran on the BBC for something like ten years' worth of Saturday nights, and on every single show he got into drag and did a sketch that ended with the aforementioned catchphrase.

"They don't like it up 'em!"

"They" refers to the Germans. "It" was the end of a bayonet wielded by one of the squadron of plucky pensioners in the sitcom *Dad's Army*. This comedy about the British Home Guard in

WW2 went off the air in the late 1970s but still shows up in prime time, and its plethora of catch-phrases still pop out of the mouths of the populace.

"You'll like this. Not a lot, but you'll like it."
Catchphrase associated with diminutive magician Paul Daniels

Cockney Rhyming Slang
"It Don't Arf Pen and Ink in Here!"

If you were born within hearing distance of the clanging sound of the big bells of Bow (the Church of St. Mary le Bow in Cheapside, East London), you can consider yourself an authentic cheeky Cockney, an Eastender—whose appellation according to the *Oxford English Dictionary* derives from "cock and egg" after a misshapen, unappetizing-looking egg—and you therefore consider mangling the language a birthright.

A second plausible derivation of the word can be found in *Webster's New Universal Unabridged Dictionary:* London was referred to by the Normans as the Land of Sugar Cake (Old French: *pais de cocaigne*), an imaginary land of idleness and luxury. By extension, the word "Cocaigne" referred to all of London and its suburbs and over time had a number of spellings: Cocagne, Cockayne, and, in Middle English, Cocknay and Cockney. The latter two spellings could be used to refer to both pampered children and residents of London. To pamper or spoil a child was "to cocker" him.

While Cockney rhyming slang was first heard in the fifteenth century, it came into its own in the 1800s when street traders and criminals alike used it as a means of covert communication to conceal illicit practices. No longer solely the jungle telegraph of the underworld, rhyming slang lives on as a cultural barometer. If your name is prominent enough to be utilized as a rhyme for something mundane, you are an individual of significant impact and we should all raise our Britneys to you. Britney Spears. Beers.

Church of St. Mary le Bow
Credit: The Hoberman Collection/
Alamy

Adam and Eve

Rhyming slang for believe

"Would you Adam and Eve it?"

Apples and pears

Rhyming slang for stairs

Barnet

Hair (Barnet Fair—a popular fair
held in High Barnet, now a
borough of London)

Battle cruiser

Rhymes with boozer, which
means pub

Bin lid

Rhyming slang for child
(lid = kid)

Boat

Rhyming slang for face (boat
race)

Boracic

Rhyming slang for skint or broke
(boracic lint = skint)

Brahms

Rhyming slang for drunk (Brahms
and Liszt = pissed)

Bristols

Breasts (from Bristol City, rhymes
with titty)

Brown bread

Rhymes with dead. Unfortunately
for those who have been advised
by their GP to give up white
bread.

Bubble
Rhyming slang for laugh (bubble bath = laugh)

Bubble
Rhyming slang for Greek (from Bubble and Squeak, a purportedly edible fried delicacy made from cabbage and potato)

Calvin Klein
Wine

Camilla Parker Bowles
Rolls, as in Royce

China
Rhyming slang for friend (China plate = mate)

Cobblers
(1) rhyming slang for balls (Cobbler's awls = balls) (2) nonsense

Colonel Gadaffi
Café

Corn beef
Deaf

Cream crackered
Rhyming slang for tired (cream crackered = knackered)

Currant
Rhyming slang for both son, as in male child, and the scurrilous British tabloid the *Sun* (currant bun = son, the *Sun*)

Daisy roots
Rhyming slang for boots

David Gower
Rhyming slang for shower, Gower being the famous England cricketer renowned for his ability to take a shower

Dicky bird
Rhyming slang for word

"I haven't heard a dicky bird from her."

Dog and bone
Telephone

"I'm on the dog and bone, you cow!"

Down the Swanie
Down the drain, as in best-laid plans going astray

"I was on a promise for some rumpy pumpy tonight but that's gone down the swanie."

Duchess

Rhyming slang for wife (Duchess of Fife = wife)

Emma Freuds

Modern-day rhyming slang for hemorrhoids, name taken from the writer, broadcaster, and great-granddaughter of Sigmund Freud, best known these days for being Richard Curtis's girlfriend

Frog and toad

Rhyming slang for road

"Why did the chicken cross the frog and toad?"

Gary Glitter

The anus, rhymes with shitter, sad fate for the glam rock star turned runaway nonce

Ginger

(1) redhead (2) rhyming slang for queer (Ginger beer = queer)

Gypsy's kiss

Rhyming slang for piss

"I'm just going out for a quick gypsy's."

Half inch

Rhyming slang for pinch, meaning to steal something

Hampstead

Rhyming slang for teeth (Hampstead Heath = teeth)

Have a butcher's

Rhyming slang for have a look (look = butcher's hook)

Iron

Homosexual (iron hoof = poof)

J. Arthur

Wank, British term for masturbation (J. Arthur Rank = wank). J. Arthur Rank was a famous entrepreneur who ran chains of bingo halls, dance clubs, and cinemas. (also **Jodrell**, derived from the telescope Jodrell Bank)

Jack and Jill

Cockney rhyming slang; some say it means pill, some say bill. Thus, after a visit to your GP, you can say, "This Jack and Jill's a bitter Jack and Jill to swallow."

Jacobs

Rhyming slang for testicles (Jacobs' Cream Crackers = knackers)

Jam jar

Rhyming slang for car

Jimmy Riddle

Urinate (from piddle)

Joanna

Rhyming slang for piano

Joe Baxi

Rhyming slang for taxi

Khyber

Rhyming slang for asshole (Khyber pass = arse)

Laurel and Hardy

Bacardi

Lee Marvin

Starvin'

Mince pies

Rhyming slang for eyes

Mutt 'n' Jeff

Rhyming slang for deaf

On your todd

Rhyming slang for being alone (Todd Sloane = alone), after the famous British jockey. Famous in Britain, anyway.

Pen and ink

Rhyming slang for stink

Plates

Rhyming slang for feet (plates of meat). Most feared phrase by British grandchildren visiting their grandparents:

"I've been walking around all day, little ones. My plates are killing me. Give them a rub, will you?"

Porkies

Lies (from Porky Pies)

Radio Rental
Rhyming slang for crazy, mental
(Radio Rental, the name of a chain
of TV hire shops in the UK)

Raspberry
Many uses: rhyming slang for
nipple (raspberry ripple), cripple
(raspberry ripple again), and fart
(raspberry tart)

Richard
Rhyming slang for fecal matter
(Richard the Third = turd)

Rosie Lee
Rhyming slang for tea

Rub-a-dub
Rhyming slang for pub

Ruby Murray
Rhyming slang for curry

Scooby (doo)
Rhyming slang for clue

*"I don't have a Scooby why he did
that."*

See you Oscar
See you later (Rhymes with Oscar
Slater, the Glasgow man accused
of murder. Even the efforts of
Arthur Conan Doyle couldn't
save him from the gallows; later
evidence cast doubt on his guilt.)

Septic tank
Rhyming slang for American
(septic tank = Yank)

Soapy
Rhyming slang for trouble (Soapy
bubble = trouble)

Steves
As in Steve McQueen. Jeans.

Sweaty sock
Rhyming slang for a Scottish
person (sweaty sock = jock)

The Sweeney
Rhyming slang for the police.
Sweeney Todd = Flying Squad,
specialist branch of the metro-
politan police, inspired a 1970s
TV series of the same name filled
with angry shouting violent cops.

Syrup
Wig (from syrup of figs)

Tea leaf
Thief

Thrupenny bits
Rhyming slang for tits; often
abbreviated to "froops"

Titfer
Hat (from tit for tat)

Tomtit
Rhyming slang for shit

"Just nipping out for a tomtit."

Tony Blair
Flares

Trap
Mouth (from pony and trap)

Trouble and strife
Rhyming slang for wife

Two and eight
Rhyming slang for state, as in panic

*"He's got himself in a right two and
eight over that old slag."*

Vera Lynn
The name of the famous wartime
sweetheart now known chiefly as
rhyming slang for gin

Whistle
Apart from the usual meaning,
rhyming slang for suit (whistle
and flute)

Wick
As in "You get on my…," you are
an annoying person; wick is short
for Hampton wick, rhyming slang
for prick, however the phrase can
be used to bemoan the insensitiv-
ity of a female irritant. Con-
versely, the accusation "You get
on my tits" can also be hurled at a
male. That whole "Men Are from
Mars, Women Are from Venus"
thing doesn't seem so smart now,
am I right?

Winona Ryder
Not, as you might imagine, "she's
got stolen goods hidden inside
her," but rather the more
innocuous cider

Polari
Fantabulosa!

Gay slang language, which saw greatest use in the London of the 1950s and '60s (and was revived briefly in the '90s by Morrissey via his *Bona Drag* album and characteristically unhummable song "Piccadilly Palare"). Ironically, while fear of exposure and subsequent shame, ruin, and incarceration at the hands of an intolerant society forced Britain's gay population to lead secret lives and converse in a code concocted from Romany, Yiddish, and Italian, that same intolerant society was laughing itself silly at that same code. One of the most popular BBC radio comedy series of the 1960s was the surreal sketch show *Round the Horne,* which surrounded the stentorian tones of host Kenneth Horne with a repertory company of baying grotesques who conversed almost entirely in double entendre. Two of the show's most popular regulars were Julian and Sandy, a camp double act played in the broadest possible fashion by gay comic actors Kenneth Williams and Hugh Paddick, who conversed in Polari to the extent that terms introduced in their segments made their way into the national vocabulary where they remain to this day. A brief list follows. Take a vada:

Bijou
Small

Bona
Good

Camp
Effeminate (originated from the acronym KAMP: Known As Male Prostitute)

Kenneth Williams (right) in *Carry on Matron*
Credit: Pictorial Press/Alamy

Cottage
Public toilet

Crimper
Hairdresser

Glossies
Magazines

Khazi
Toilet

Mince
Walk

Naff
Bad (acronym, meaning Not
Available For Fucking)

Onk
Nose

Polari
Chat, talk

Trade
Sex

Troll
Walk about (in search of trade)

Vada
Look, see

Clothes
Dedicated Follower of Fashion

Balaclava
Wool hat covering the head

Braces
Suspenders

Cagoule
Windbreaker

Dinner jacket (or DJ)
Tuxedo

Jumper
Sweater

Mac (short for mackintosh)
Raincoat; additionally, **dirty mac**, a worn and besmirched raincoat synonymous with perverts and gentlemen of the tabloid press

Off the peg
Off the rack, ready to wear

Plimsolls
Sneakers

Polo neck
Turtle neck

Shell suit
Shiny track suit, favored uniform of chavs

Strides
Trousers

Turn-ups
Pants cuffs

Vest
Undershirt, also **singlet**

Waistcoat
Vest

Windcheater
Windbreaker

Collective Terms
Mob-Handed

Auntie
The BBC (from Auntie Beeb)

Building society
Savings and loan association

Fleet Street
The press, because the majority of the nation's newspapers were produced there. The term remains, even though most of Britain's daily and weekly publications have relocated to a new location known affectionately as the Gutter.

Harley Street
London street renowned for its array of murderously expensive doctors, therapists, and plastic surgeons

Savile Row
London street renowned for its array of world-class tailors

Whitehall
Refers to the government because so many government offices are situated in the vicinity

The Yard
Scotland Yard

Compliments
Sweet as a Nut

Belter
Enthusiastic opinion of a person, place, or thing

"She's a belter, that Mary Kate Olsen."

The Business
All-purpose compliment that can be applied to any given person, object, work of art, or foodstuff regarded in a positive manner

"These coconut macaroons are the business!"

Butter up
Flatter and compliment

Corker
Similar to **belter**

"That Ashley Olsen, what a corker!"

Diamond geezer
A good, solid, reliable, salt-of-the-earth type

"That little bloke who works down the Chinky? Diamond geezer, gave me extra rice."

Full of beans
Bursting with energy

"He's full of beans, isn't he, considering he's just got the one leg?"

Gayer
Not unaffectionate description of a homosexual male

"It's your mate, the gayer."

Good nick
Good condition, generally used to describe an item for sale, such as a used car that is about to fall to pieces

Guv
Or guv'nor, short for "governor"; deferential form of address to an elder or superior, unless it's used by a contractor to a householder, in which case it's bristling with unspoken contempt

Jammy
Lucky

"You jammy bastard!"

Mucky pup
Affectionate term for a dirty child

My old son
Affectionate form of address between two males, neither of

A mucky pup
Credit: Matt Harris photography/ Alamy

whom need necessarily be related

Scrub up well
Clean up well, dress up smartly, in comparison to scruffy normality

Snazzy
Well dressed, smart, and attractive

Soft lad
Affectionate northern term for a soft-hearted, sentimental person

Sweet as a nut
Okay, fine, things are great

The Bill
The police, named after William Wilberforce, the member of Parliament who put forward the original proposal for a national police service (also **the old bill**)

Bizzies
Liverpudlian term for the police

The Filth
The police

Grass
Police informer; the unstoppable —and, within these pages, frequently name-checked—British sitcom, *Only Fools and Horses,* recently spun off a series in which one of its characters became a police informer and then swiftly fled to a new life in the countryside. It's called *The Green Green Grass.*

Have your collar felt
Get arrested

The Filth
Credit: Janine Wiedel Photolibrary/ Alamy

Identity parade
Lineup

Manor
Territory occupied by criminals but patrolled by aggressive Cockney TV policemen who regard them as trespassers on their property

"You're on my manor, sonny."

Nark
Police informer (also **grass, supergrass**)

Nicked
Arrested

The Old Bill
Slightly affectionate but at the same time contemptuous method of conferring familiarity on the police

Panda car
Small police car

Peelers
Archaic term for police derived, like **bobbies**, from Sir Robert Peel

Plod
Policeman (from PC Plod of Enid Blyton's *Noddy* books, beloved of children the world over)

Rozzer
Policeman

Scuffers
Police

Summons
Citation

Supergrass
The supermodels of police informers. Tattletales who give up names and information so incriminating they capsize vast criminal empires. And then live in fear. Super-fear, to be exact.

Truncheon
Nightstick

Criminal
"Dodgy!"

Banged up
Be put in prison

Banged-up
Incarcerated

Bent
Crooked

Bung
Bribe

Diddle
Cheat someone

Do a bunk
Run off, avoid paying a bill, play truant

Fair cop
A legitimate arrest

"It's a fair cop, guv'nor, you caught me with the swag."

Fit-up
Frame *"I didn't do it! I was nowhere near, it's a fit-up!"* (also **stitch-up**)

Flash Harry
A confident, well-dressed, smooth-talking character, usually untrustworthy, probably criminal. May or may not actually be called Harry. (also **Jack the Lad**, a cheery young whippersnapper with such an infectious joie de vivre; it's impossible to resent

him as he laughingly relieves you of your valuables.)

Had your card marked

Been warned. Derived from football [soccer] where a player who commits a foul is issued a yellow or red card, and has his name noted in the referee's notebook.

"You've already had your card marked, don't come around here looking for trouble."

Her Majesty's pleasure

A term in prison

It fell off the back of a lorry

A subtle way of telling the potential purchaser that the cheap DVD he's about to buy is stolen without the seller actually using those incriminating words, so that, when the DVD refuses to eject or play a disc, the purchaser has no legal recourse. The chump.

Kerb crawler

Disreputable individual known for driving at a leisurely pace in the vicinity of a high school or a red-light district and clearly up to no good

Kiddie fiddler

Pedophile

The nick

Prison

Nonce

Pedophile

On the fiddle

Being involved in illegal activities

Porridge

Prison sentence

Previous

A criminal record ("He's got previous"). Compare U.S. usage: priors, as in "He's got priors."

Ramraider

Unimaginative criminal who robs a store by crashing his car straight through the window, then clambering inside and stuffing his pockets with the swag

Scrumping

The boisterous adolescent pursuit of stealing apples from orchards

Shed load

A large amount

"Ere mate, wanna buy one of them plasmatic TVs, I've got a shed-load in the garage. Fifty quid the lot!"

Shopped

Informed on (also **grass**)

Stitch up

Con someone

Well in it

In trouble

Casualty ward
Emergency room

Collywobbles
An upset stomach, a feeling of
nervousness

The dreaded lurgy
Any unspecified ailment that
allows the victim to take time off
work

Gammy
Injured or diseased part of the
body

"I've got a gammy leg!"

Gandhi's revenge
Effect of brutal foreign food on
delicate British constitution,
usually ending in a horrifying
bout of diarrhea; equivalent
American usage, "Montezuma's
revenge"

Jab
A shot, immunization

Long-sighted
Farsighted

Nits
Head lice

*"Don't bring yer nits into my nice clean
house, ya wee midden!"*

Operating Theater
Operating room

Peaky
Feeling a little under the weather

Piles
Hemorrhoids

The runs
Diarrhea

The screaming abdabs
(1) a fit of nerves (2) the reaction of the delicate British constitution to any kind of overly spicy foreign meal

The squits
Diarrhea

Turn
Onset of illness, usually foreshadowed by dramatic announcement from notorious hypochondriac

"I'm having one of my turns."

Double Meanings
Don't Slag Me, You Slag!

A good seeing to

(1) a painful beating (2) sexual intercourse

"I gave her a good seeing to and anyone who says different gets a good seeing to, right?"

Blag

(1) to steal (2) to get away with something

"I blagged my way in."

Boiler

(n) furnace; (adj) derogatory term for female presumed to be of loose morals

Bottle

Courage, guts. Also used in the phrases **Lost His Bottle**, a derisive description of someone whose courage failed him at a defining moment, and **Bottled It**, a terse but equally snide dismissal of someone who cultivated a thuggish exterior but, when it came to the crunch, was a sniveling sissy.

Cack-handed

(1) left-handed (2) clumsy

Dander

(1) a leisurely stroll

"I'm going out for a wee dander by the riverbank."

(2) temper

"Don't get your dander up."

Done up like a kipper

(1) caught in the act (2) left twisting in the wind as a result of an act of treachery or extreme deviousness by another party

Duff up

(1) beat up (2) **duffer**, meaning foolish or old person (3) rubbish

Gob

(1) mouth (2) spit

Going to see a man about a dog

(1) going to the bathroom (2) noncommittal answer hiding true destination

Having it

Fully enjoy oneself, as in **having it large**, or, **have it off**, or, **have it away**, meaning sexual intercourse

How do you do

(1) how are you? (2) expanded to "This is a fine how do you do," the phrase refers to a complicated and potentially serious situation.

Kiosk

(1) newsstand (2) telephone box

Nosh

(n) food and drink; (v) to eat

Oi!

(1) form of greeting, usually delivered by cheerful Cockney characters (2) declaration of aggression, delivered with equally bloodcurdling effect by enraged policemen and rampaging soccer hooligans (3) postpunk subgenre: loud, fast, brutish tuneless row produced by skinheads, brought into disrepute by its affiliation with the UK's Nazi-inclined National Front

The P45

The termination of a relationship or a period of employment. A P45 is the official form given to someone on their dismissal from his or her place of employment and explains tax details that are required by a future employer. Equivalent American usage: pink slip.

Ponce

(1) a contemptible person (2) an effeminate male (3) to freeload

Rank

(1) disgusting (2) taxi stand

Slag

(1) an unattractive female of loose moral standing (2) an insult

"Why did you slag off that slag?"

Sod

(1) a derogatory term for an objectionable, annoying person (2) a sympathetic term for someone who bears the brunt of constant bad luck

"Poor sod."

(3) something that is problematic

"We had a sod of a time getting that old soak out of the basement."

(4) sod's law; like Murphy's law: anything that can go wrong will go wrong. All derived, however inscrutably, from "sodomite."

Steaming

(1) drunk (2) angry (3) moving quickly (4) adjective of abuse

"You great steaming nit."

(5) exciting new trend in teenage crime where large mobs of youth move in on lone victims in buses or subways, surround them, and cause violent distress

Stick

(1) abuse

"He gave me a lot of stick about my collagen injections."

(2) intolerance

"I can't stick him and his collection of porcelain figurines."

Sticky wicket

A cricket-derived reference to an awkward or embarassing situation

Stonking
(1) something impressively huge
(2) something excellent (also
stonker)

Stuffed
(1) bothered

"I can't be stuffed going to the boozer."

(2) "get stuffed," go away (3)
"Stuff one's face," eat greedily.

Top
Good (as opposed to **top
oneself**, meaning commit
suicide)

Wee
(1) to urinate (2) small, tiny
(chiefly Scottish)

Well
Apart from the usual meaning,
adjective meaning "very"

"I'm well pleased about that result!"

Wellie
(1) short for Wellington boot,
based upon Hessian boots worn
and popularized by Arthur
Wellesley, first Duke of Wellington, and fashionable among the
British aristocracy in the early
nineteenth century. Also known
as a "gumboot."
(2) exhortation

"Give it some wellie, you wally!"

Whopper
(1) something large

"Is it big? It's a whopper!"

(2) a lie

*"He told me it was big. That was a
whopper."*

Drugs
Sorted for E's and Whizz

Caned
Drunk or, more popularly,
stoned

Charlie
Cocaine

Gak
Cocaine

"He's been at the gak."

Gear
Drugs, formerly clothes, formerly
'60s Mod expression meaning,
roughly, "cool"

On one
Acting crazed, often as a result of
stimulant intake

Sorted
Expression of satisfaction,
specifically used to celebrate the
acquiring of enough drugs to get
through the weekend (also
sound, sound as a pound)

Charlie
© James Lange/PYMCA

Drink

"Pissed as a Newt!"

Bevvied
Intoxicated

Bitter
A type of beer; also a state of mind brought on by consumption of beer

Bladdered
Drunk

Boozer
The pub, the bar

Chucking out time
11 PM. Close of business in British bars. The reason that drinking grows increasingly more frenzied as the night goes on. A source of nightly amazement and crushing disappointment to British drinkers who can't believe the landlord really wants them to leave. A time of night beloved by the proprietors of Turkish kebab establishments whose profits soar from the custom of the victims of chucking-out time, most of whom are far too drunk to have any awareness of what they're actually eating.

Get that down your neck
Have a drink

Half
Half pint of beer

Half cut
Drunk

Lager
Beer

Mullered
Drunk (possible reference to mush-mouthed Cockney charac-ter actor Arthur Mullard)

Murder
Thirst, hunger

"I could murder a pint."

The Offy
The off-license (equivalent to an American convenience store licensed to sell beer and liquor)

Old soak
Drunkard of long standing

On the lash
Out getting drunk

Paralytic
A state of intoxication so advanced that you are unable to access any of your motor functions and have to be carried out of the bar and folded into the back of a waiting taxi while drool dribbles from your mouth and urine stains your crotch. Not that I remember it happening that way . . .

Plastered
Drunk

Plonk
Cheap wine

Rat-arsed
Drunk

Paralytic
Credit: Photofusion Picture Library/ Alamy

Ribena

Black currant drink popular with children; also a smashing addition to many cocktails where it's known by the more exotic moniker "black." (Doesn't rum and black sound more exciting than rum and Ribena? Actually it probably doesn't if you've never heard of Ribena before.)

Scrumpy

A rough cider made in the west of England and consumed mainly by farmhands who enjoy its therapeutic effect on their repressed hatred of the nearby townsfolk and their hoity-toity ways

Shandy

Half-beer, half-lemonade, very refreshing; not to be confused with **hand shandy**, referring to the act of masturbation, which is also very refreshing

Shout

A round of drinks

"Put your hand in your pocket and buy the drinks, it's your shout!"

Skinful

Too much to drink

Sloshed

Drunk

Snifter

A small drink of alcohol, a shot

Snockered

Drunk

Sozzled

Drunk

Squiffy

Slightly drunk, tipsy

Wallop

Any powerful intoxicant, particularly beer

Wellied

Drunk

Contemporary Conversation
Geezer!

A hiding to nothing
You're in a no-win situation.
Loser.

Arse over tit
Fall over so spectacularly clumsily
that it can't be brushed off in a
cool, self-mocking "I-meant-to-
do-that" way

At the sharp end
Where the action is

Batch
Short for "bachelor"

The Big E
Dump an unwanted romantic
partner once the bloom is off the
rose (E standing for "elbow")

The big I am
Someone very full of themselves

Billy No Mates
A person with no friends (also
Nobby No Mates: he doesn't
have any friends either. They
should hang out!)

Blinding
Fantastic

Booze Cruise

Cheap day trip by ferry across the English Channel to France to stock up on cheap alcohol, which is about all the French are good for . . .

Brass monkey

Extreme cold

"It's cold enough to freeze the balls off a brass monkey!"

A freezing cold monkey
Credit: Papilio/Alamy

Bricking

Lose control of your bowels under extreme stress, probably derived from "brick shithouse"

"I bricked myself when I saw all these chavs coming down the frog and toad."

Bumf

An aggregation of useless clutter, whether junk mail or actual physical crap that takes up space but which you can never bring yourself to get rid of because you think labeling yourself a pack rat adds some charming quirk to your character; derived from the seventeenth-century term bum-fodder, itself a term for toilet paper. So ask yourself, would you keep a pile of your old, used toilet paper around for sentimental reasons?

Chocka

Description of a crowded environment, derived from "chockablock"

"The pub was chocka last night."

Color supplement

Magazine included with the Sunday papers

Come again

Please repeat what you just said.

Comprehensive school

High school

Cracking

Excellent (also **cracker**: sexually attractive female)

Dialing code

Area code

The dog's bollocks

An exclamation of extreme praise

"My dog's bollocks are the dog's bollocks!"

Dosser

Homeless person

Drop you right in it

Get another person in trouble, whether deliberately or by accident

"You dropped me right in it when you told the old woman I lost her dog."

End of

Curt and contemptuous abbreviation of "end of story." Generally used by the overconfident and egocentric to close an argument and crush the chances of any possible comeback.

"I don't care what you think. Iran is the capital of Iraq. End of!"

'Er indoors

Jokey, but in actual fact somewhat cowed and fearful reference to one's wife. Made popular by the lovable TV con man Arthur Dailey, played by actor George Cole on the 1980s series *Minder*.

Feck!

Euphemism for "Fuck!" Originated in the TV show *Father Ted*.

Fill your boots

Help yourself, go ahead

"There's enough mashed potato for everyone. Fill your boots!"

GBH of the earhole

Being verbally assaulted by the sheer volume of an opponent who might not have a better argument but who is capable of keeping up the yelling ad nauseam.

"I heard you the first five hundred times. Stop giving me GBH of the earhole!"

Go off on one
Get annoyed

Goss
Short for "gossip"

Graft
Work

Gutted
Upset and disappointed; most frequently employed by heartbroken UK football [soccer] fans after their hopes of international glory are once again dashed.

Handbags at dawn
A feud or disagreement between two individuals whose meek demeanors or unimposing physicality renders them completely ineffective. "It's handbags at dawn between those two" is a spectator's derisive overview of

such a conflict. The sissy-boy smackdown between Hugh Grant and Colin Firth in both *Bridget Jones* movies is a perfect illustration of "handbags at dawn" taken to its logical conclusion.

Handsome
Very good, a satisfactory turn of events

"Wossat? I won a fiver on the pools? Handsome!"

Having it large
Ubiquitous declaration of hedonism in the club scene of the '90s

"We're having it large! No, I don't know what time I'll be home, Mother."

Having kittens
Panicking

Innit
Meaningless all-purpose suffix; performs the same function as "Know what I'm saying?"

"And I wasn't looking where I was going so I banged right into that door, innit?"

Knock it on the head
Stop doing something, give something up

Kushty
Excellent, fine, okay (another expression that came to prominence due to consistent exposure on the BBC sitcom *Only Fools and Horses*)

Leg it
Run

Lost the plot
Gone mad, also gone mental, also simply said or done something extremely stupid

Mad for it
Very enthusiastic. Expression originated during the Manchester clubs, drugs, and music scene of the early 1990s. Because they were all mad for it, see?

Massive
English hip hop fans' self-conscious attempt to pass themselves as a posse representing their hood (see, for example, Ali G's Staines Massive)

Mockney
Professional Cockney; sometimes an actor or comic exaggerating his East End roots, or sometimes an individual with an upper-class upbringing dressing, talking, and acting in a manner calculated to convince the world of his authentic Cockney roots. I wish I could think of a good example but *cough* Guy Ritchie *cough* my mind is blank.

Muck around
Waste time

Nappy Valley
Description of a district where the majority of the population consists of young couples with preschool children

Near the knuckle
Potentially offensive sexual content, whether it be a joke, a TV show, or a film

Nice little earner
A (usually illegal) get-rich-quick scheme

No joy
No luck

Papped
Being stalked, harassed, and surreptitiously photographed by the paparazzi

Paps
Paparazzi

Pram-face
Disdainful description of young working-class female for whom the future promises nothing but the certainty that she'll be pushing her children around in a pram before she's left her teens

Reccy
Short for reconnaissance, check something out

Redundant
Fired from a job, made unemployed

Roister doister
Cheerful, boisterous person

"How you doing, you old roister doister?"

Sarky
Sarcastic

Scanties
Panties

Sharon and Tracey
Disparaging term for loud, vulgarly attired working-class females

Shift
Move quickly

"You should have seen him shift when it came time to buy a round."

Shufti
Look

"Have a shufti at that curry. Does that look like a dead mouse?"

Sick as a parrot
Horribly disappointed; most frequently employed by heartbroken

UK football [soccer] fans after their hopes of international glory are once again dashed.

The skip
Dumpster

Skive
The avoidance of work, laziness. (This may offer a belated explanation as to why Bananarama titling its debut album *Deep Sea Skiving* was so hilarious.)

Sod that for a game of soldiers
It's not worth bothering about.

Sound as a pound
Very good, excellent, especially given the excellent exchange rate currently enjoyed (as this book is being written) by the British pound sterling versus the sick-as-a-parrot American dollar

Spark out
Pass out

Spark up
Light a cigarette or joint

Splash out
Spend money recklessly, emboldened by an upcoming special occasion rather than a windfall

Throw a wobbler
Throw a fit or tantrum

"She didn't half throw a wobbler when she heard he'd been having it away with some old boiler!"

Upmarket
Upscale

What's he/she like?
Puzzled reaction to confusing or eccentric behavior. Carried over to the United States by Neneh Cherry's hit song "Buffalo Stance" and its line "What's he like anyway?"

White Van Man
The driver directly behind you who sits behind the wheel of a

white van cursing you out for your lack of driving abilities; whether you were too cautious to speed through the lights or you pulled away too recklessly, the White Van Man is always right behind you and he's always furious.

Wrinklies
Dismissive term for parents or people over forty who conspire to suppress the kids

You what?
I beg your pardon?

Vintage Vocabulary: Quaint Expressions That Are Still with Us
"Not on Your Nelly!"

A bit of a do
An occasion (party, wedding reception, banquet, Royal wedding)

A chin wag
A chat

A cock and bull story
Long, rambling, unbelievable anecdote

A face like fizz
A miserable expression. Similarly, "A face like a slapped arse" connotes an even more pronounced brand of melancholy.

"He was stood there with a face like fizz. I said, 'What's wrong, did your cat die?' I should be a psychic me, I'm that good."

A fair crack of the whip
A chance to participate in a desirable activity

"I've given you a fair crack of the whip, now if you wouldn't mind returning my lawn mower in the state you originally found it."

A good innings
A long and productive life (derived from cricket)

A mug's game
A foolish undertaking that will leave everyone involved much the worse for wear

"Gambling is a mug's game."

A right one
An expression of embarrassment

"And it turns out there is a difference between pre- and postoperative transsexuals. I felt like a right one, I can tell you."
Also, **A right 'nana**, which means exactly the same as **A right one** with the embarrassment factor being so excruciating that the individual responsible for the faux pas feels it appropriate to compare himself to an abbreviated banana

A rum do
A confusing incident

A turn-up for the books
An unexpected but not un-pleasurable occurrence

A wet weekend in Wigan
A way of describing a person or event as being as boring as watching paint dry that maligns a sleepy town in the northwest of England that happens to be famous for its obsessive appreciation of vintage American soul music, for being the UK's wrestling capital, and for producing the legendary hard candy Uncle Joe's Mint Balls. Sounds pretty exciting to me!

Afty
Afternoon

Agriculture show
County fair

"And the answer is— a lemon"
Phrase used by hardhearted teachers to belittle students who, through no fault of their own, may be flustered at the prospect of having to speak up in front of a classroom full of vicious little bastards. Or maybe they hadn't done their homework and if that was the case then they obviously had a credible excuse so to belittle them in front of an entire class-room is completely inexcusable. Never happened to me. No sir. Never.

Anticlockwise
Counterclockwise

Apples and oranges

The pointless comparison of two things that have little do with each other

"Coconut macaroons and kidney donors? You're talking apples and oranges there, mate."

As the actress said to the bishop

Seventies sitcom version of "That's what she said." Turns innocent phrase into something dripping with innuendo, coined in 1930 by author Leslie Charteris in *Enter the Saint*:

"'I must go get my little Willy out of the sun before he turns red and I have to rub cream all over him,' as the actress said to the bishop."

At sixes and sevens

Feeling awkward and confused

Baccy

Tobacco

The back of beyond

The sticks, the boondocks (unfortunately rejected alternate title for movie starring Angelina Jolie and Clive Owen)

Badge

Button

Bagsie

Stake your claim for something. U.S. equivalent: "I call dibs."

Bald as a coot

Bald. As in completely bald. Hairless on the head

Bang goes sixpence

Self-deprecating reference to a person—usually of Scottish descent—and his reluctance to part with money

Bang out of order

Do or say something entirely inappropriate

"You were bang out of order when you told my mother she had a face like a bulldog chewing a sock full of wasps."

The baths

Public swimming pool

Be mum

As in "I'll be mum," i.e., I'll pour the tea; disgraceful stereotype perpetuating the myth that a woman's natural state is one of compliant servility. Having said that, you won't catch me being mum.

Beaver away

Work hard

"He's been beavering away on that report for hours."

Beggar's belief

Beyond belief

Believe you me

Believe me. The pointless addition of the extra "you" suggests a Welsh derivation.

Bespoke

Custom-made

Best of British

Good luck!

Better than a poke in the eye with a sharp stick

Another way of reminding an ungrateful recipient that the paltry amount he is receiving for, say, compiling a list of British slang, is better than nothing at all

Bint

Derogatory term for woman, derived from the Arabic. Figures.

Bird

Term for female, comprehensive in the 1960s and '70s, rarely used in a nonironic sense in these more enlightened times (also **dollybird:** complimentary '60s term for miniskirted swingers)

Biro

Ballpoint pen

Bit

Abbreviated from the cheery compliment "she's a bit of all right," the less complimentary "bit of rough," and the even less complimentary "bit on the side"

Bloke
Guy

Bloody Nora!
Exclamation of surprise, shock, or anger

Blot one's copybook
Spoil an otherwise unblemished record through an uncharacteristically thoughtless deed or shoddy workmanship

Blue pencil
Censor something

Bob's your uncle
Satisfied suffix to a sentence meant to denote that the speaker's grasp of his subject is unimpeachable and no argument is necessary. Origin: In 1887 Robert Arthur Talbot Gascoyne-Cecil, third marquis of Salisbury, appointed his nephew Arthur Balfour to the position of chief secretary for Ireland. The appointment was controversial, given Balfour's previous low profile, and accusations of nepotism—"Bob's your uncle!"—accompanied his tenure in the position

Boffin
Expert, usually in science, generally bald and blinking through huge glasses, sporting a lab coat and peering with some concern at the test tube that is about to explode and alter his DNA, causing him to mutate into a savage manifestation of his long-repressed id

Boom boom!
Verbal rim shot, used by comics to drive home the punch line of a successfully delivered one-liner or, even more commonly, to act as a life-support system for a gag that expired the instant it was uttered. Most associated with Basil Brush, a puppet fox who has proved one of the BBC's most durable comedy stars.

Brackets
Parentheses

Brass tacks
Getting down to the unvarnished truth, the real nitty-gritty

British summer time
Daylight savings time

Basil Brush
Credit: Pictorial Press/Alamy

Building society
Small bank (such as a credit union)

Bully for you
Sarcastic reaction to another's good fortune

"I just got a promotion, a huge raise, a company car, an expense account, and a hot secretary!" "Bully for you."

Bumbag
Fanny pack

Busman's holiday
A vacation spent doing the exact same things you do when you're at work

Butter no parsnips
From the phrase "fine words butter no parsnips," meaning "Flattery or flowery language is in itself useless, only actions count"

Caff
Café

Carry the can
Take the blame

Chance your arm
Take a risk

Cheery-bye
Chirpy mutation of cheerio and good-bye, employed by mad old grannies and aunties in a way that suggests that, while they're happy that you deigned to visit them in their twilight years, they can never

wait to see the back of you and
your condescending ways

Chief cook and bottle washer

Someone in charge of running a
household, evolved into something of a self-deprecating term to
denote one's position in the
household; often employed by a
husband to communicate that he
will occasionally deign to involve
himself in what he regards as
women's work

Chinwag

A cheery, gossip-filled
conversation

Chips

French fries

Chop-chop

Hurry up. Borderline offensive,
especially when directed at a
person of Asian extraction.

Chuffed

So filled with self-regard at your
general excellence that you puff
up with pleasure. You idiot.

Clapped out

Broken down, devoid of energy
or life, applicable to machine or
person

Clobber

Clothes

"Close your eyes and think of England"

Pearl of wisdom passed down
from mothers to daughters
petrified at the horror awaiting
them on their wedding night

Clunk-click

Catchphase taken from a 1970s
commercial emphasizing the
necessity of wearing a seat belt at
all times. After displaying brutal
cautionary footage of eviscerated
drivers and passengers who set
out on their trip without belting
up, the commercial's narrator,
ebullient British DJ Jimmy Saville,
would utter the phrase "Clunk-
click every trip" as a euphemism
for wearing the seat belt. Even
though the commercial is an
antique, the phrase continues to
resonate

Cock-a-hoop
Extremely pleased, over the moon

Cocked a deaf 'un
Turned a deaf ear

Cock-up
Mistake (alternate usage, **A cock-up on the catering front**)

Codswallop
Ancient sporting competition in which rivals beat each other senseless using the carcasses of day-old fish as weapons. I'm totally kidding! In fact, I'm talking codswallop, slang for nonsense that sounds like it's been in existence since the dawn of time but dates back only as far as the 1960s.

Cop it
Get into trouble

"I'm going to cop it for shattering the old man's cherished porcelain figurine!"

Cor
Expression of surprise, shortened from "Cor Blimey" or "Gor Blimey," which are themselves corruptions of "God Blind Me"

Cotton reel
Spool of thread

Counterfoil
Ticket stub

Crikey!
Another exclamation of surprise

Crimble
Cheery abbreviation of "Christmas," probably originated by John Lennon when he said "Garry Crimble to You" on a 1963 Beatles fan club disc (also know as **Crimbo**)

Curate's egg
Something that is neither all good nor all bad, a mixed bag. Derived from a nineteenth-century cartoon in *Punch,* the long-running humor magazine and dentist's waiting room staple, in which a young clergyman is served a bad egg while a guest at his bishop's breakfast table. When asked his opinion of the egg, rather than offend he blurts out, "Parts of it are excellent." You had to be there.

Daddy Longlegs
Crane fly

Daft as a brush
Silly

Darby and Joan
An affectionate and slightly condescending way of describing an elderly married couple. Coincidentally, my own parents are named Darby and Joan.

Deco
A look (have a deco, have a look)

Deffo
Definitely

Dilly dally
Waste time

Doddle
Something easy; compare U.S. equivalent: cakewalk

Dog's dinner
As in, "All dressed up like a . . ."; contemptuous description of a person convinced that his outer appearance will compensate for a lack of breeding. The frightful oiks.

Doing a ton
Driving at 100 miles per hour in a car or on a motorcycle

Doings
Nonspecific term for person or thing whose name you can't quite place, usually employed by forgetful parent to irresponsible child

"Your friend . . . doings called at two in the morning." "You left your . . . doings blasting all night. Some of us have work in the morning, you know . . ."

Don't get your knickers in a twist
Don't get worked up. U.S.: Don't get your panties in a bunch.

Don't give a monkey's
Don't care

Don't teach your grand-mother to suck eggs
A withering rejoinder from someone of advanced age and

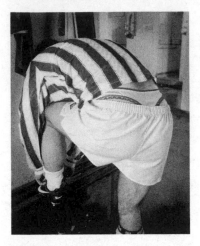

Knickers
Credit: ImageState/Alamy

experience to a callow youth who might be foolish enough to attempt to teach them something they already know

Dotty
Harmlessly eccentric, slightly wandered (also **batty, barmy**)

Down in the dumps
Miserable, depressed, lachrymose, inconsolable. Entirely unlike myself.

Draughts
Checkers

Dress circle
Mezzanine (in theater)

Dressing gown
Bathrobe

Drop a clanger
Make a faux pas

Dummy
Pacifier (yet the title of the Vin Diesel film was not changed to *The Dummy* on its UK release)

Early doors
Anachronistic phrase used by pub landlords to describe the period of peace and quiet that lasted up until around 5:30 in the afternoon before the doors opened and the army of parched customers charged in and began drinking themselves into oblivion

Effing and blinding
Swearing

El vino collapso
Cheap disgusting wine that nevertheless gets the job done

Ex directory
Unlisted number

Fair to middling
Average; a favorite expression of those who shrink from expressing any kind of enthusiasm

"How have I been since winning the lottery? Fair to middling."

Fireplug
Fire hydrant

First-year student
(also known as undergraduate)
Freshman

Fit for the knacker's yard
Exhausted to the point where death is welcome (knacker's yard meaning roughly the same thing as the U.S. usage of glue factory)

Fleece
Shearling

Flex
Electric cable

Flutter
A gamble made by someone who is not a serious gambling addict

"I like to have a bit of a flutter on the ponies every now and then"—or so he/she claims.

Forty winks
A nap, brief period of sleep

Fringe
Bangs

Full stop
Period

Funfair
Amusement park

Gallivanting
Carousing, getting up to high jinks

Gander
Look around, take a look

"Would you take a gander at what she's wearing?"

Geegees
Horses. Used by wide-eyed children and hardened gamblers.

Gen up
Get information, study

Gercha!
Cockney term of amused disbelief; corruption of "Get out of here!"

Ginormous
Big; combination of "gigantic" and "enormous"

Give over
Stop

"Give over, we've all heard the story about you having three months to live . . ."

Go down a bomb
Perform spectacularly; the exact opposite of "to bomb" in the American sense

Go like the clappers
Move as quickly as is humanly possible

Gobsmacked
Amazed

Gone for a Burton
Dead. A Royal Air Force term to describe what happened to a missing pilot.

Good nick
Good condition

Gordon Bennett!
Exclamation of disbelief, thought to be a reference to the high-living playboy James Gordon Bennett Jr., who, among his many accomplishments and outrages, introduced polo to the United States. His Paris Hilton–like tabloid ubiquity in the late 1800s led to his name becoming synonymous with incredulity.

Got the hump
Depressed, in a bad mood, feeling miserable after prolonged exposure to "My Humps" by the Black Eyed Peas

Green Shield Stamps
Tokens given away with super-market purchases and at gas

stations. Shoppers in the 1960s and '70s avidly stuck their Green Shield Stamps in their Green Shield Stamp books. Once they'd filled the books with stamps, they took them to the Green Shield Stamp Centre where they redeemed them for domestic items, such as toasters, garden furniture, and toys. The Green Shield Stamps achieved such national popularity that supermarket prices rose to cover the costs of printing and distributing them, thus hastening their extinction at the start of the 1980s.

Greenfingers
Green thumb

Gubbins
Layman's term for anything technical he doesn't understand

Gurn
Pull faces. Once a competitive countryside sport where old toothless farmhands tried to contort their leathery visages into the most grotesque expressions. The advent of ecstasy as a social lubricant caused gurning to become a common sight at most raves.

Guts for garters
As in, "I'll have your . . ."; military slang used to strike fear into the hearts of raw recruits by brutish parade-ground tyrant attempting to break down their individual spirits and mold them into a crack fighting machine or, then again, simply to cause them to soil themselves for his amusement.

Half a mo
Wait a minute

"Hands off cocks, on with socks!"
Raucous wake-up call designed to shock schoolboys, Boy Scouts, and army recruits out of their dreams and into action. The female equivalent, "Hands above the bedclothes!" is less well established due to insufficient catchiness.

Hard cheese
Bad luck

He doesn't know he's born
Disappointed appraisal of someone who takes his good fortune for granted

He knows what's what
He knows what's going on

He's off his rocker
He's crazy (also **he's off his trolley**)

Hemming and hawing
Prevaricating and filibustering in a futile attempt to cover up the fact that you are completely ill-prepared and have no idea what you're talking about

Higgledy-piggledy
Uneven, a mess, all over the place

High Street
Main street, main drag

Hoarding
Billboard

Hobson's choice
No choice at all

Hold the phone
Wait a minute. U.S. equivalent: Hold your horses.

Homely
Simple, unpretentious

Horses for courses
To each his own

Hue and cry
Cause a commotion

Hunky-dory
Fine, okay, very good. Excellent, in fact, if applied to the hunky-dory album named *Hunky Dory* by David Bowie. Less so if in reference to the patchy *Funky Dory* by Rachel Stevens.

I should coco(a)
I should say so

"Going down the pub?" "I should coco!"

"I'll give you a ring"
"I'll call you"

I'll go to the foot of our stairs
An expression of extreme surprise and befuddlement. Comparable to the American "I'll

be a monkey's uncle." And
equally nonsensical.

In the pudding club
Pregnant; still with us in the
abbreviated "In the Club," which,
of course, inspired the 50 Cent hit
of the same name

Interval
Intermission

Inverted commas
Quotation marks

It'll all come out
in the wash
Sooner or later the truth will be
discovered

Jack Robinson
Someone or something who
appears with incredible speed.
Derived from the phrase "Before
you could say Jack Robinson,
there he was."

Jasper
Wasp

Jiggery pokery
Untrustworthy behavior

Jim jams
Pajamas

Joe Bloggs
The average guy, the man in the
street. U.S. equivalents: Joe Blow,
Joe Six-Pack, Joe Pantoliano.

John Bull
Everyman representation of the
nation, the American equivalent
being Uncle Sam

Jotter
Notebook

Jumble Sale
Rummage sale; yard sale

Keen as mustard
Very enthusiastic

Keep mum
Keep quiet; be cautious with
information you impart.

Famously used in a World War II security slogan:

"Be like dad, keep mum."

Keep your hair on
Stay calm

Keep your pecker up
Stay cheerful, don't be down-hearted. Also used by women as an exhortation to an under-performing sexual partner, I've been told.

Kerfuffle
A fuss. Lately a catchphrase on the popular sketch comedy show *Little Britain*.

"What's all the kerfuffle about? I'm only two hours late. She hasn't had the baby yet, has she? So shut up!"

Kip
Sleep, especially in the sense of a nap, in which case one might say, "I need a wee kip," where the U.S. equivalent might be "I'm gonna try to get forty winks."

Kith and kin
Friends, neighbors, and family, one's nearest and dearest

Knees-up
Party, possibly derived from the cheery old standard "Knees up, Mother Brown"

"We've just been to a right-old knees-up."

Knocked for six
To be dealt a severe blow (cricket expression, where a six is the highest score the batter can make on one bowl)

Know your onions
Possess a full and comprehensive knowledge of a subject

Lacquer
Hairspray

Ladder (in tights)
A run in one's tights

Laundrette
Laundromat

Lead on, McDuff
Cheerful request to another to guide the way; misquoted from Macbeth's dying words, "Lay on, MacDuff, and damn'd him that first cries, 'Hold, enough!'"

Leader
The main editorial in a newspaper or publication

Left luggage
Baggage room

Left, right, and center
A thorough search

"I've looked left, right, and center for that bit of string!"

Lift
Elevator

Lose the rag
Lose one's temper

Lost property office
The lost and found

Lucky dip
Grab bag

Marriage lines
Marriage certificate

Maths
Math. Everytime a British viewer sits down to watch an American movie or TV show, there will come a time when an on-screen character will deliver the line "Do the math" and the UK audience member will unleash a corrective "sss."

Medium wave
AM radio

Mind your p's and q's
Be on your best behavior

Moggy
Cat. The origin of the word "moggy" is not a corruption of the word "mongrel," as many believe. It was first recorded in 1911 and was possibly derived from "Maggie," "Margie," or "Mog," all short forms of the female name Margaret.

"More tea, vicar?"
Parody of genteel response to an accidental expulsion of gas in a formal gathering

Muck in
Join in and help someone finish a task

"Don't just stand there watching me grafting my arse off—muck in, you lazy cow!"

Mucker
Friend

Nappie
Diaper

Naughts and Crosses
Tic-tac-toe

Niggling
Nagging doubt

Nipper
Child

Nobbled
Tampered with, damaged

Not a sausage
Nothing; to come up empty-handed, bereft of so much as a single sausage

Not backward at coming forward
Someone who is bursting with confidence

Not cricket
Unacceptable behavior

Not half!
Absolutely!

"Do you want to go down the boozer?" "Not half!"

Not on your nelly
No way

Not to be sneezed at
A gift or opportunity not to be passed up

Odds and sods
Bits and pieces (also known as **bits and bobs**)

Off you pop
Affectionate dismissal

Oh my giddy aunt
Oh my goodness, oh my God

Old banger
Aged car in perilous state of repair

Old lag
Person of advanced years

On the cadge
Begging

On the cards
Something that is very likely to occur. In the United States, "in the cards" is the equivalent expression.

On the razzle
Having a good time

On the up and up
Trustworthy, accurate

Order of the boot
Fired, dismissed, downsized

Out of puff
Out of breath

Paper round
Paper route

Park yourself
Sit down

Patience (the card game)
Solitaire

Pavement
Sidewalk

Pegged out
Exhausted (similarly **pegged it:** died)

Pelican crossing
Walk/Don't Walk sign

Perspex
Plexiglass

Peter out
Run out of energy

Pig's ear
Incompetent execution of a relatively simple task; also a delicious repast

Pillar box
Postbox; pillar boxes are, of course, the bright red, cast-iron edifices that appear, along with equally bright red double decker buses, in American movies to establish that the action has suddenly relocated to the UK.

Pinny
Apron

Pinta
A pint of milk; testimony to the power of advertising, the Milk Marketing Board's "Drinka Pinta Milka Day" drummed this slogan into the subconsciousness of the Great British Public.

Piss it up the wall
Spend money in a reckless fashion

"Cor blimey, I had fifty quid and I pissed it up the wall last night."

Piss like a race horse
As in, "I need to . . ."; to give expression to an almost unbearable urge to urinate

Plaiting fog
As in, "You'll have more chance . . . ," a way of puncturing a fondly held delusion

"You'll have more chance of plaiting fog than getting me to sit through another Steven Seagal straight-to-DVD movie. Unless it's Belly of the Beast 2. That first one was crazy . . ."

Plaster
Band-Aid

Pleased as punch
A state of happiness, meaning derived from the creepy, sadistic puppet Punch, whose carved wooden rictus never varies in expression when he is beating his

partner Judy to a pulp in front of an audience of happily cheering prepubescents

Poly bag
Plastic bag

Pop your clogs
Die

Premium bond
Government bond

Pukka
First-rate, very good (Indian origin, commonly used by lovable Cockney TV chef Jamie Oliver)

Pull a fast one
Gain an unfair advantage

Pull someone's plonker
Pull someone's leg. And by leg I mean leg. Not what you were thinking. Cheeky monkey.

Pull the other one, it's got bells on
I don't believe what you're saying to me, and in addition I like the sound of bells

Punt
Gamble

Queer Street
Be in trouble

"The missus is going to be looking for that fifty quid I pissed up the wall. If she don't get it I'm gonna be in Queer Street."

Rabbit
Talk (also **natter, palaver**)

"He doesn't half like a rabbit that one, talk the hind legs off a donkey, he would."

Rare as hen's teeth
Something very rare. Like hen's teeth. Because hen don't have teeth, except maybe in Chernobyl.

Recorded delivery
Certified mail

Resident
Hotel guest

Right as ninepence
Correct

Ring up
Call someone on the phone

Rota
Duty roster, work schedule

Rough it
Live without luxuries. Compare the same expression in the United States, where it means "to lose high-speed Internet access for five minutes just as I was in the middle of downloading porn."

Rubber
Eraser. If a British person asks to borrow an American rubber, he or she is not necessarily a sexual pervert. However, do keep alert.

Rubbish
Trash

Rumbled
Discovered

"She rumbled me when she heard me talking to that other bird on the dog and bone."

Running around like a blue-arsed fly
Rushing around in a frantic hurry while in actuality achieving very little

Sack
To be fired, or to fire someone, from a job

"I had to give him the sack."

Scarper
Run

"The old bill are coming. Scarper!"

School term
School semester

Schtum
Silent

Secateurs
Handheld pruning shears

Secondary school
High school

Second-year student
Sophomore

See you anon
See you at a later date

Sent to Coventry
Shunned, ignored. Probable origin: the hasty exit in 1642 of Charles I from London to Royal-friendly Coventry after parliament discovered his Catholicism, sowing the seeds of the bloody English civil war and the scarcely better song of the same name by the Clash.

Shank's pony
To walk

Shipshape and Bristol fashion
Everything in order

Silly buggers
Someone indulging in horseplay and malarkey with scant regard for the feelings of others

"Ignore him, he's just playing silly buggers. He's not really planning on shooting anyone."

Skew-whiff
Crooked, misaligned

Skivvy
A maid, cleaning woman

Sleigh
Sled

Slog your guts out
Work very hard

Small potatoes
Something trivial and insignificant, a trifling amount of money (alternate term **small beer**)

Smidgeon
A small amount (diminutive **smidge**). U.S. equivalent: a tad.

Smoothie

Seventies term for a pickup artist with a well-rehearsed catalog of lines. Roger Moore is the epitome of Smoothiehood.

Snuff it

Die. Compare U.S. expression, "kick the bucket."

Sod's law

Like Murphy's law, the overwhelming probability that whatever can go wrong will go wrong

Song and dance

To make a song and dance of something is to create unnecessary drama over a mundane situation, thus diverting attention and blame away from your personal culpability.

Spanner

Monkey wrench

Spiffing

Excellent, first-rate

Spiv

Cheery con man, petty crook, most prevalent during WWII (alternate term, **wide boy**)

Sponge bag

Toiletry bag

Sprog

Baby, young child

Starkers

Naked

Stick your neck out

Take a risk or put yourself on the line for someone; generally used prefacing an expression of disappointment

"I stuck my neck out for you and this is how you repay me? You're fired, Mother!"

Stone

Measurement of weight (one stone = 14 pounds)

Strewth

Exclamation of surprise, derived from "God's truth"

"Strewth, mate, one minute he was right here talking to me, the next he was nowhere to be seen."

Strike a light!
Expression of surprise (also, **stone me**)

"You ate how many pieces of macaroon? Strike a light!"

Stroll on!
Expression of disbelief

"You paid how much for that wooden clock? Stroll on!"

Suited and booted
Well dressed

Surgery
Doctor's office

Swing the lead
Wasting time

Swings and roundabouts
Six of one, half a dozen of the other

Swipe
Steal

Swish
Posh, fancy

"This hotel is a bit swish, isn't it?"

Swiz
Expression common to British schoolchildren in the 1950s and '60s when they gave voice to disappointment over being cheated or conned

"I spent all that money on those sea horses and this is all I get? What a swiz!"

Swot
Student who studies to the exclusion of any other activity or social intercourse. Compare U.S. usage: nerd or wonk.

Ta
Thank you

Take a running jump
I do not believe what you are telling me. Compare U.S. equivalent: take a long walk off a short pier.

Talent
Attractive person or group of people

"There's a lot of talent in this boozer, my old son, looks like I'll be copping off tonight."

Talk the hind legs off a donkey
Supposedly complimentary description of someone in love with the sound of his own voice

Tannoy system
Public address system (used mainly in schools)

Tart up
Smarten up (in the sense of dress up)

Teat
Nipple on baby's bottle

That takes the biscuit
That beats everything I have ever heard

That's a turn up for the books
That is an unexpected occurrence. Compare the much more elegant American usage: "That's one for the books"

The cut of your gib (or jib)
A positive comment on the character of another. Derived from seafaring slang. The foresail, or jib, of a ship, indicates its character to the sailor.

The dickens
A common expression for the devil, used centuries before the birth of Charles Dickens, the author, or Kim Dickens, the actress.

The full shilling
In possession of all your mental faculties. Most common usage:

"He's not quite the full shilling."

The great unwashed
Unappetizing description of the masses

The pictures
Films

The short and curlies
As in, "I was caught by . . .":
being found out and held
accountable for your actions by
someone so sure that you'll be
unable to lie, cheat, bluff, beg, or
fight your way out of the situation
that it's almost as if he or she has
a tight grip of your pubic hair;
alternatively, it could mean that
someone has a tight grip of your
pubic hair.

The whole kit and kaboodle
All your worldly possessions

The willies
Butterflies in the stomach,
growing fears. A fairly successful
export in the United States, where
it's used most often in reference
to horror movies of the slasher
subgenre.

*"They say he's nice enough guy but
something about him gives me the
willies. Could be the leaking baps
he keeps in his backpack, I don't
know . . ."*

Thick as a brick
Even more lacking in common
sense than someone who is
considered to be thicker than two
planks; someone who is rigid in
his or her conviction about an
indefensible belief, i.e., a favor-
able reappraisal of Jethro Tull is
right around the corner

Thump
Negative expression

*"Are you looking forward to visiting the
dentist?" "Am I thump! Last time the
bastard took six of me teef out!"*

Tickety-boo
Everything's going exceedingly
well

Tin
Can (tin opener = can opener)

To boot
An added bonus

*"I'll give you a slap in the face and a
clip round the ear to boot if you don't
mind your manners, sonny Jim!"*

To come a cropper

To become the victim of actual bodily harm; to stand by as carefully laid plans go astray. Derived from horse-riding argot wherein to "fall neck and crop" means that the horse has hit the ground with both neck and crop.

To ferret out

A determined attempt to get to the truth, even if it means inserting live ferrets down a suspect's trousers in order to do it

To thumb one's nose

To express contempt and defiance for authority by the pressing of thumb against nose and the subsequent rebellious wiggling of fingers

To tide someone over

A modest act of generosity designed to help someone through a period of hardship until a more permanent form of salvation arrives

"This box of coconut macaroons is just to tide you over until a kidney donor shows up."

Tom, Dick, and Harry

Paranoid generalization for the pack of lawless thugs lurking in wait to rape and pillage if the door isn't locked, gas isn't turned off, TV turned down. Usually used by aggrieved parent to irresponsible child.

"Close the door. Any Tom, Dick, and Harry could walk right in off the street and rob us blind!"

Tombola

Lottery in which tickets are drawn from a revolving drum and the lucky winner gets to choose from prizes the caliber of a soiled oven glove, a wooden kettle, or a clock missing the number 8

Toodle pip

Pre–WWII method of saying good-bye, used frequently in films by upper-class twit characters

Tootle

Driving at a leisurely speed

"Just out for a tootle in the old banger."

Transport caff
Roadside café

Trundle
Move slowly and exhibit imminent signs of falling over, like a
very young or very old person

*"Just saw granddad trundling down the
stairs, looked as if he was about to keel
over."*

Tuppence ha'penny
Two and a half pennies in non-
decimalized currency; another way
to dismiss something as negligible

*"He drives up here in that tuppence
ha'penny car of his, I didn't know
where to look."*

Also used in conversation as
"tupenny ha'penny."

Two shakes of
a lamb's tail
Do something promptly

Umpteen
Innumerable, a lot

*"You had umpteen chances, and you
blew the lot."*

Uncle Tom Cobley and all
A phrase meaning everyone you've
ever met, including individuals to
whom you have only the most
tenuous acquaintanceship

*"I thought it was just going to be me
and a few mates. I walked in the door
to find me old feller, 'im next door,
Uncle Tom Cobley and all!"*

From the old folk song
"Widecombe Fair."

Unit trust
Mutual fund

Up the duff
Pregnant

Up the wooden hill
to Bedfordshire
Going to bed

Up to snuff
Meet all requirements, considered
satisfactory

Use your loaf
Use your brain, think

Video Nasty

An '80s classic. The widespread acceptance of the VCR into the British household created a demand for product so ravenous that zero-budget exploitation classics like *Cannibal Holocaust* and *I Spit on Your Grave* nestled in high-street video stores alongside items intended to entertain the entire family. A crusade to protect the nation's impressionable youth from these movies, dubbed "Video Nasties" by Mary Whitehouse, the indefatigable self-appointed scourge of the airwaves who spearheaded the march to clean up the screens, led to the passing of the 1984 Video Recordings Act. Suddenly, retailers stocking titles like *The Evil Dead* were liable for prosecution. Ironically, the whole reason Mrs. Whitehouse and her National Viewers and Listeners Association even became aware of the Video Nasty was because the distributors of *Cannibal Holocaust,* on the lookout for some free publicity, contacted her in the guise of an outraged citizen, furious that such filth was allowed to fester in her local video store.

Waffle

Obfuscate

"He waffled on for a good half hour before he made his point."

Walking papers

As in, "I gave him his . . ."; to be fired from a job or to be dumped by someone. Or both, if that office romance went sour.

Wendy house

Child's playhouse

Wet the baby's head

Celebrating the birth of a child by participating in a lengthy and raucous drinking spree

What's that got to do with the price of eggs?

Reply to an irrelevant statement

What's what

How things are

Whip-round

Collection. When office workers are cajoled into contributing toward a cash gift for a retiring colleague or a get-well-soon card or a wedding present or anything that the little voice inside them is screaming "No!" to, they're taking part in a whip-round.

Who's he when he's at home?

Inquiry as to the identity of someone about whom the interrogator has already formed a low opinion. Also used to ask the meaning of a fancy word with the implication that whoever used the word was trying to impress the listener with his or her erudition.

Witter on

Incessant babbling

"He doesn't half witter on, bless him."

Wizard!

Dated expression meaning great or excellent (also **top hole**, **spiffing**)

Wonky

Faulty, badly assembled

"Don't sit down too hard, the chair's a bit wonky."

Wotcha

A greeting employed mainly by cheeky Cockney types

Yonks

Years

"Haven't seen her in yonks."

Argy Bargy
Argument; a British way of saying "argument schmargument"

Bairn
Baby, small child (Scottish)

Balls-up
To have failed at a given task in a humiliating manner; the phrase cock-up means exactly the same thing.

Barry
Splendid, good (Scots)

Bogging
Disgusting, smelly (Scottish)

Brand-new
Excellent, of high quality (the warmhearted Scots again!)

Braw
Good (Scots)

Ceilidh (prounced "kay-lay")
A fun event involving the drinking of beer and the throwing of oneself about to Scottish country dances with names like the Gay Gordons and the Slosh

Chap on the door
Knock on the door (chiefly Scottish)

Chib

Scottish term that can be either a noun or a verb but is equally fearsome. If an enraged Scot attacks a potential victim with a chib, he will be brandishing a non-projectile weapon, a razor, a lead pipe, a broken bottle, a piece of wood. The chib is always something that has been modified from its original intended use to double as a weapon. A gun, knife, sword, or light saber are not chib-worthy. If an enraged Scot attacks a potential victim minus a chib, he will be assaulting his adversary armed only with his fists, feet, and, most important, his forehead. He will be administering a chibbing.

Chuck

Term of endearment most commonly used in the north of England, pronounced "Chook," rhymes with "book"

Clarty

Stinking, revolting (Scottish)

Cock

Expression of Cockney affection, derived from "Cock Sparrow." Used between males as substitute for "mate." Most common usage:

"Wotcher cock," i.e., "How are you doing, my good friend?" Cock has declined in popularity in recent years.

Div

Sometimes affectionate, sometimes pejorative Liverpudlian term for a person of low intelligence

Donkey's years

A long time

"I haven't seen you for donkey's years."

There's probably an ass joke in there somewhere, but I can't be arsed.

Ecky thump

Exclamation of shock and surprise delivered in a mock Lancashire accent and employed to parody natives of the north of England, much in the way the slack-jawed yokel on *The Simpsons* paints an unflattering portrait of its inspiration. Originated on *The Goodies,* a surreal slapstick TV show created by college chums of the Monty Python team, where it was a term for an ancient Lancastrian form of martial arts. (My memory may be failing, but someone died laughing at a *Goodies* episode, possibly the ecky thump one.)

Eejit

Chiefly Irish pronunciation of "idiot"

First foot

A Hogmanay tradition: to ensure good luck for the coming year, a dark, male stranger carrying a lump of coal should be your first visitor after midnight.

Give it laldy

Perform a task with cheerful enthusiasm (Scottish); also **give it some welly**

Give over

From the north of England; can mean "stop it," "shut up," "I don't believe you" (much like "shut up!" now has a multitude of meanings in American usage)

Glaikit

Wear a vacant, moronic, slack-jawed expression (Scottish)

Going 90 to the dozen

Speaking—or performing any activity—very fast (Scottish/ Irish)

Good crack

Chiefly Irish for a good time, which might involve smoking good crack

Grog

Spit and, trust me, the Scots *love* to spit (Scottish)

Gutties

Rubber-soled sports shoes, trainers (Scottish)

Happen

Northern for "maybe"; often used in movies by monosyllabic locals who are all complicit in the town's dark secret but present a stoic face to the newcomer whose quest for the truth will explode all the years of lies

"Do you know a place where a weary traveler can rest for the night?" "Happen I do. Happen I don't."

Haver

Dither, fail to come to a decision (Scottish, rhymes with "waver")

Head-the-ball

An unstable person. Head is pronounced "heed" in the local vernacular (Scottish/ Irish)

Hogmanay

Scotland's apocalyptic alcohol, violence, and fireworks–filled New Year's Eve celebration

Hoo-ha

Fuss

"Don't make a hoo-ha out of it, I'll buy you a new cat."

Jobby

Lump of excrement (chiefly Scottish)

Kecks

Trousers (Liverpudlian)

Keech

Another lovely Scottish euphemism for excrement; to make it even more pleasant, the "ch" is pronounced phlegmily (like the Scottish stretch of water "loch")

Ken

Know (Scottish)

"You've got a wee bit of jobby on the sole of your shoe." "I ken."

Kinnell

Northern expression of anger or surprise (corruption of "fuckin' hell")

Knock back

Rejection, refusal, barred entry; can be applied to anything from an establishment to a woman; also referred to as a KB

"I tried to buy her a drink but she gave me a KB."

La'

Liverpudlian term of endearment applied to young men, corruption of "lad" (most famously used by the band the La's or, as clueless DJs occasionally refer to them, the L.A.'s)

Leccy

Liverpudlian slang for electricity, specifically their electricity bill, specifically their reluctance to pay same

Look you
Look. The Welsh again and their superfluous *you*s.

Made up
Very happy (Liverpudlian)

"I'm made up that they didn't come and take the telly away."

Mam
Northern way of saying "mum" (also **Our mam**)

Messages
Shopping (chiefly Scottish)

Midden
A slob, a dirty, scruffy, unkempt place or person, like Pigpen from *Peanuts* (Scottish-Irish)

Mind!
Northern British expression meaning watch out, be careful (from mind yourself or mind out)

Minging
Scottish-Irish expression meaning filthy, smelly, disgusting, unpleasant

Mithering
Northern slang for whining or interfering

No mark
Worthless person (Liverpudlian origin)

North of Watford
Dismissive term used by cocky Londoners to describe the impoverished, foul-smelling wasteland that, to their mind, is the rest of country

Nowt
Nothing (Scottish/northern)

Numpty
Scottish expression for idiot

Oggy Oggy Oggy! Oi Oi Oi!
Battle cry of Welsh rugby fans; familiar to Americans because of its use by Catherine Zeta-Jones when she won the Academy Award for Best Supporting Actress for *Chicago* and felt the urge to declare to the watching world that she was sharing her

moment of triumph with all of Wales. Sadly, all of Wales couldn't share her excitement as it was too busy dying of embarrassment.

On the burroo
On the dole, claiming unemployment (Scottish)

Our kid
Affectionate Liverpudlian term for younger sibling

Owt
Yorkshire term meaning "anything"

"He didn't tell us owt."

Palaver
Commotion

"He came in here shouting at the top of his lung, starting a big palaver."

Pan in
Break or disfigure (Scottish)

"You keep talking like that, you're going to get your face panned in. Not by

me. But someone's going to do it. Probably."

Pech
Breathe loudly and phlegmily (Scottish, rhymes with "blecchh")

Peelie-wally
Pale, sickly looking (chiefly Scottish)

"He's a wee bit peelie-wally-looking, doctor." "That's because he's dead."

Sassenach
Derogatory Scottish term for the cowardly, lily-livered English

Skelp
Scottish expression meaning a slap administered by a parent for a truculent youth's own good

Skoosh
Fizzy drink (Scottish)

Square go
Scottish term for a fight

"You have insulted my family name. Prepare for a square go!"

Stoater
Someone or something of high quality (Scottish)

"See him, he's a wee stoater, so he is."

Stocious
Drunk (chiefly Scottish)

Stood
Standing

"I've been stood out here in the rain all day!"

Stowed out
Full to capacity (chiefly Scottish, pronounced like "cowed out")

"The pub's stowed out. Help!"

Summat
Northern British for "something"

"There's summat not quite right about that lad."

Wazzock
West Country term for "idiot"; loses its sting when delivered in that thick country burr. That way you don't know how much they hate you big-city folks.

Wean
Baby/child (chiefly Scottish, pronounced "wayne"), derived from "wee one"

Your man/woman
Chiefly Irish for a man or woman

"See your man over there, he's going to get a belt in the chops if he doesn't get out of the way of the TV."

Fighting Talk
A Bit of a Barney

A carry on
A loud argument or commotion

A good rollicking
Tell someone off

"I gave him a good rollicking."

A punch up the bracket
A punch aimed in the region of
the nose and mouth

*"You'll get a punch up the bracket if I
catch you looking at my pint!"*

A tanner
Sixpence

Barney
Argument leading to violence

Bolshy
Hostile and argumentative.
Corruption of invented slang
from Anthony Burgess's novel
A Clockwork Orange, in which the
author concocted a convinc-
ing futurist British slang that
mixed Russian, Cockney rhyming
slang, and sheer neologisms to
great effect. In the book,
"bolshy" was used in its original
Russian derivation, to mean
"great big," or some approxima-
tion thereof.

Brass neck
Cheek, impudence, nerve, sass
(seemingly a term of admiration
but rarely applied without
disdain)

Claret
Blood (from the color of claret, which is bloodlike)

Clout
Hit someone with the intent of knocking some sense into them rather than causing them physical damage

Dead leg
Knee someone on the side of the thigh (a common assault during the school years, very painful). U.S. version: charley horse.

Ding dong
Fight

"I don't know what he said but one minute we were just having a bit of a natter and the next there was an almighty ding dong, fists flying, the whole bit!"

Do one
Leave

Done over
Beaten up

Down the tubes
An expression indicating that an object or situation is no longer functioning or proceeding according to plan

"I can't pick you up at the airport. The motor's gone down the tubes."

Get knotted
A brusque dismissal

Go off on one
Throw a fit

Go spare
Become unreasonably angry

Hard nut
Aggressive, tough person

He gets on my wick
He annoys me to the point that I may have to chastise him in a brutal fashion

I don't give a monkey's
I don't care

Knuckle duster
Brass knuckles

Lace into
Attack, either verbally or
physically

Lamp
Hit somebody

"I lamped him."

Leave it out
Stop that

Lose your rag
Lose your temper

Make it snappy
Hurry up

**Make mincemeat
of somebody**
Beat someone up

Mob handed
Be part of a group, usually
looking for trouble

Nut
Head butt

Offer someone out
Challenge someone to a fight.
Equivalent to the standard
U.S. challenge, "Let's take it
outside."

On my uppers
Flat broke, destitute

Paddy
A rage or tantrum

"Don't get in a paddy."

Put a sock in it
Be quiet

Rollocking
A chewing out, being torn off a
strip

Ruck
Fight

Shirty
Angry

"Don't get shirty with me, mate!"

Shove off
Go away

Shut your cakehole
Shut your mouth

Sling your hook
Leave, go away

Stick one on someone
Hit someone

"He looked at me funny so I stuck one on him. Turns out he was blind, but still, he was asking for it."

Stitch that!
Soccer hooligan war cry shouted while delivering a head butt or similar act of violence to an adversary, rival, or innocent passerby; a contemporization of the more genteel cry to arms "Take that!"

Strop
A bad mood

"Don't throw a strop just because you got a bad pint."

Also, **stroppy.**

Throw a wobbler
Similar to throwing a strop but somehow more petulant; the sort of behavior you might expect from a truculent D-list celebrity expecting to be instantly seated at a restaurant even though s/he hasn't made a reservation

To box someone's ears
To give them a slap around the head for misbehaving

The V-sign
The infamous "up yours" gesture achieved by extending the first and middle fingers at the same time as raising the hand upward; now sadly supplanted by the middle finger

Well 'ard (well hard)
(1) Someone who is tough

"You don't wanna get in a ruck with that geezer, he's well 'ard."

(2) An exclamation of enthusiasm

"You got in a ruck with that geezer and you gave him what for. Well 'ard!"

What for

Speak roughly to someone or threaten to deal with them physically

"I gave him what for."

You're having a laugh

You're enjoying a joke at my expense and this is causing me increasing displeasure that will result in physical confrontation . . .

Food
Scrummy!

A slap-up meal
A very expensive and extravagant feast

Aubergine
Eggplant

Bangers
Sausages

Bap
Bread roll

Bath Oliver
A dry biscuit eaten with cheese

Brekky
Breakfast

Bubble and squeak
Economical method of reheating the soggy, stone-cold leftovers from a previous meal. Generally, the ingredients most friendly for recycling are mashed potato, cooked cabbage, and cold beef. The whole mess is chucked in a pan spitting with hot fat and left to sizzle for twenty minutes, during which time, legend has it, the morsels make a sound that could be interpreted as bubbling and squeaking. Shortly after having excused yourself from the dinner table, you will make a similar sound.

Butty

Staple of the British lunchtime diet, a roll slathered with butter and then made irresistible with the artery-hardening addition of fat, greasy rashers of bacon, french fries, and fried egg. No wonder the UK is regarded as the sick man of Europe. Having said that, I could murder a chip butty right about now.

Chicken Tikka Masala

AKA the most popular restaurant dish in the UK. Invented, urban mythology has it, by a Bengali chef working in my hometown of Glasgow, Scotland, who was confronted by an irate, gasping customer who demanded gravy to pour on his tandoori chicken. The quick-thinking chef whipped open a tin of Campbell's soup and came up with a bright-orange concoction simultaneously spicy and mild enough to satisfy the British appetite without wreaking havoc on its digestive system. Whether or not the stirring tale of its origins is entirely true, it's an undeniable fact that millions of prepacked Chicken Tikka Masala meals are rung up on supermarket tills every day. Not only that, but UK retailers do a booming trade in CTM chips, pizzas, pasta sauce, and sandwiches. The only possible ending for such a success story would be that British food companies are now turning fast profit importing Chicken Tikka Masala to India, which, of course, is exactly what's happening.

The Chinky

The Chinese restaurant where you get your takeout

Cornet

Ice-cream cone

Cornish pasty

Cornwall's gift to the British appetite; a pouchlike creation constructed from short pastry, baked, stuffed to bursting with meat and vegetables, and sealed across the top. Mmmm good!

Courgette

Zucchini

Crayfish

Crawfish

Crisps
Potato chips

Crumble
Fruit pies with crumbly topping made from flour and fat

Cutlery
Silverware

Demerara sugar
Light brown cane sugar

Digestive biscuits
There are many varieties of biscuit lining the British super-market shelf but just as the Hoover has come to be synony-mous in the mind of the con-sumer with all vacuum cleaners, so the plain and sturdy digestive is the foodstuff of choice for Brits to eat with—and sometimes dunk in—their tea. McVitie's, the company behind the nation's most loyally consumed diges-tives—famously advertised in the 1970s by Monty Python's Graham Chapman as the "sugges-tive digestive"—has maintained its supremacy with the iPod of digestive biscuits, the sleek and luxurious Hob-Nob.

Din dins
Cutesy way of referring to dinner, often used when summoning animals or small children to the table

Eccles Cakes
Tasty, unpretentious raisin-stuffed cakes first produced in the district of Eccles in Salford, Manchester; during the period when the Puritans gained power, they banned Eccles Cakes, attributing pagan significance to their mouth-watering flavor.

Elevenses
Midmorning tea or coffee break

Gobstopper
Jawbreaker

Hamper
Gift basket stuffed with yummy edibles

High tea

Early dinner in late afternoon, not to be confused with afternoon tea, which is a serving of tea or coffee and a microscopic sandwich in the middle of the afternoon

Horlicks

Milky hot drink, made by adding hot water to powder, which produces an almost immediate soporific effect. U.S. equivalent: Ambien.

Hovis

A brand of brown bread so synonymous with the product that, for many years, Brits referred to brown bread as "Hovis," persuaded in no small part by the successful advertising campaign whose main slogan was, *"Don't say bread, say Hovis."*

HP Sauce

A staple of British dinnertime. U.S. equivalent: A1 Sauce.

Hundreds and thousands

Sprinkles on cupcakes or ice-cream cones

Ice lolly

Popsicle

Icing sugar

Powdered sugar

Jacket potato

Baked potato

Jam

Preserves

Jelly

Jell-O

Jelly baby

Baby-shaped, jelly-like fruit candy, not unlike Gummi Bears. To this day, British parents bribe and cajole their offspring with the promise that, if they're well behaved, if they finish their homework, or if they stop crying, they'll be rewarded with a very special treat: they'll be given the gift of being allowed to eat baby-shaped candy.

Joint

A piece of roast meat usually served at family gatherings on

Sundays at lunchtime, most commonly referred to as the Sunday joint or Sunday roast

Kedgeree
Breakfast dish made of fish, rice, and eggs. The prepacked version for sale in Marks & Spencer's food hall is worth the cost of a round-trip ticket.

Kipper
Smoked herring, another breakfast treat

Ladyfinger
Long, soft, sweet cake (known less embarrassingly as Sponge-finger)

Lemon cheese
Lemon curd or meringue

Lemonade
Clear, fizzy drink such as Sprite or 7-Up

Liver sausage
Liverwurst

Marrow
Squash

Mincer
Meat grinder

Muffin
Round, toasted cake of yeast dough

Oxo
A make of bouillon cubes that adds seasoning and flavor to the blandest meal

Packed lunch
Sack lunch, bag lunch

Peckish
Hungry

Pie and Mash
Minced beef and mashed potato pie; if purchased in London's East End, often served with the legendary wiggly Cockney delicacy, jellied eels

Pilchard
Fish, similar to sardine but bigger

Pip
Pit (as in something you'd find in a peach, grape, or cherry)

The Ploughman's Lunch
Stodgy and calorie-packed lunch usually consisting of a giant slab of cheese, a couple of thick slices of bread and butter, a few pickled onions. While the repast sounds like it has been a part of the British lunchtime diet for centuries, it was actually concocted in 1960 by the English Country Cheese Council as a method of forcing even more dairy products down the national gullet.

Poke
Ice-cream cone (Scottish-Irish); also **pokey hat**

Pomfret Cakes
Circular liquorice candy, also known as Pontefract Cakes

Pudding
Dessert (also known as **afters**)

Rasher of bacon
Slice of bacon

Rock
A long, thick candy cane with pink stripes on the outside and white on the inside. For many years, a souvenir of summer vacations spent in seaside resort towns such as Blackpool, Brighton, and Southend. Recipients of rock are always overjoyed by the present: to date, no one has ever finished an entire stick.

Roly-Poly
Suet pastry pudding, generally served with jam, made into a roll

Sarnie
Short for sandwich

Satsuma
Mandarin orange

Scotch egg
A hard-boiled egg wrapped in sausage meat. Delicious!

Shepherd's pie
A tasty dish made from minced beef and potatoes

Scotch eggs
Credit: foodfolio/Alamy

Smarties
M&Ms

Soldiers
Toast sliced into easy-to-digest strips; a time-honored method of making mealtime fun for difficult children

Spotted Dick
Steamed suet pudding containing currants

Squash
A fruit drink

Starter
Appetizer, first course of a meal

Sultana
Golden raisin

Sweet
Candy

Swiss roll
Jelly roll

Takeaway
Take-out food

Tandoori two-step
Reaction of delicate British constitution to spicy Indian food: diarrhea and upset stomach

Tatties
The quaint way the Scots and the Irish have of referring to potatoes

Tea
Dinner

"What are you having for your tea tonight?"

Tiffin
Light lunch

Toad in the Hole
Pork sausages covered in batter. U.S. equivalent: Toad the Wet Sprocket.

Tuck
Food (also **tuck in**: help yourself; **tuck shop**: food store specializing in candies and confectionary)

Uncle Joe's Mint Balls
Durable sugary ball of minty goodness; made in Wigan!

Underdone
Rare

"How would you like your Scotch egg, sir?" "Underdone, as always."

Welsh rarebit
Toasted cheese

Wolf one's food
Eat too quickly

"Don't wolf your food or you'll end up with a dicky tummy!"

Household
My Gaff

Aerial
TV antenna

All mod cons
Living space with all amenities
included (short for "all modern
conveniences"). Appropriated
for an album title by late-
seventies Brit-pop icons the Jam,
who fancied themselves reborn
Mods.

Answerphone
Answering machine

Bin/dustbin
Trash can

Block of flats
Apartment building

The Bog
Grim and ominous working-class
term for the toilet

Bungalow
Single-story detached house

Calor gas
Bottled gas

Chip pan
Deep fryer

Cot
Crib

Covers
Bedclothes

Digs
Rented apartment

Dish cloth
Dish rag

Doing the washing up
Doing the dishes

Drawing pin
Thumbtack

Dressing table
Dresser, bureau

Drum
Casual term for your home

"Come back to my drum, I've got some spliff and some old Gong albums. I've even got an old gong. In me drum!"

The Dunny
Toilet; derived from the English "dunnakin" and the Irish "dunnigan"

Duvet
Comforter (also, **eiderdown** or **quilt**)

Face flannel
Washcloth

Fire
Electric heater

Gaff
House; derives from the nineteenth century when a "gaff" was a slang term for a fairground or a place of cheap entertainment

Garden
Yard, backyard

Gazumped
Your offer on a house was accepted by the seller until a larger offer was made; you've been gazumped

Ground floor
First floor

Hob
Electric stovetop

Letter box
Mailbox

The Loo
Twee and chirpy middle-class term for the toilet; possibly derived from the French warning *"Gardez l'eau,"* which proceeded the hurling of the foul contents of chamber pots out of windows down onto the streets below where only the nimble of foot would escape unsplattered

Mains
Circuit breakers

Maisonette
An apartment on two or more floors

Mantelpiece
Mantel

Mezzanine
Small extra floor in between one floor and the next one up

Polyfilla
Spackle

Pouf/Pouffe
Ottoman

Pram
Baby carriage (shortened from "perambulator")

Scratcher
Bed (Scottish-Irish)

Semi
Semi-detached house

Serviette
Table napkin

Tea towels
Dish towels

Washing up liquid
Dishwashing soap

A right Charlie

A fool. Previously the term was employed as rhyming slang for "ponce" (Charlie Ronce = ponce), which can mean a freeloader, a criminal, or a homosexual. Or all three.

All fur coat and no knickers

A woman of superficial appearance and no substance

Bampot

Idiot (Scottish)

Berk

Long-surviving expression used to label someone an idiot but without much hostility behind it. For an insult light enough to have been employed on British TV from the 1960s to the present day, it's ironic to note that its origin comes from rhyming slang. "Berk" rhymes with Berkshire (or Berkely) Hunt, or cunt.

Biffer

Unattractive female

"She's a bit of a biffer but they're all the same in the dark."

Big girl's blouse

Playful way of teasing, humiliating, and emasculating a shy and sensitive young man. A father may use such a term to inspire his non–sports inclined son to throw himself more fully into a game of soccer or rugby and thus lay himself open to a crippling injury, when all he really wants to do is read his book or look at the pretty flowers.

Blackleg
Scab (someone who continues to work when all others are on strike)

Blighter
Polite way of referring to an awful, objectionable person

Bog standard
Average, mediocre

Bossyboots
Someone who orders others around

Butterfingers
Term for those who display difficulty catching or maintaining a tight grip on objects passed or hurled at them. Not the most stinging of objects except when it's hurled by psychotic gym teachers at students who never wanted to be anywhere near the soccer pitch in the first place, let alone made to play in goal where the responsibility was obviously going to be too much to handle.

Champagne Socialist
Abusive term usually employed by the tabloid press to besmirch the reputation of someone who professes to be sincere in his egalitarian beliefs but who comes from a background of privilege

Clear off
Get lost

Clever clogs (or clever boots)
Similar to "smartypants," a term that ought to connote admiration but is generally delivered in a tone that makes it clear the recipient has got above his learning and needs to remember that he's no better than everybody else

Clodhopper
Double-edged insult tainting someone as a big lumbering clumsy idiot and also casting

aspersions on their huge mis-shapen feet

Clot
Clumsy idiot

Cock a snook
Show contempt

Dago
Derogatory reference to anyone of foreign extraction, though usually reserved for Spanish or Italian

Doolally
Insane; derived from the madness that afflicted British soldiers stationed in Deolali, India

Essex girl
Derogatory term for blond, bubbleheaded, promiscuous, spray-tanned, boob-jobbed, barely clad, heavy-drinking, hard-partying female who aspires to being a soccer star's wife and who doesn't necessarily have to hail from the lovely county of Essex but it certainly adds to the stereotype if she does. Essex girl jokes have become a mainstay of British humor, a guaranteed ice breaker at social events, and a sure sign that the person delivering the gag has confused having a good memory with having a sense of humor. Purely for the sake of shining a light on a national characteristic, here are a few regrettable examples of "Essex girl humor."

Q: What's the difference between an Essex girl and a washing machine?
A: A washing machine doesn't follow you around for weeks after you've dumped your load in it.

Q: What does an Essex girl say after sex?
A: Do you really all play for the same football team?

Q: What's the difference between an Essex girl and an ironing board?
A: An ironing board's legs are difficult to get open.

Q: What does an Essex girl put behind her ears to make herself more attractive?
A: Her legs.

I'm very sorry.

Eyetie

Another popularly xenophobic term, applied to Italians

Face like a . . .

Prefix to a description of extreme unattractiveness. Examples: face like a bag of spanners, face like a bulldog chewing a wasp, face like a bulldog licking piss off a nettle, face like a dropped pie, face like a slapped arse, face like a wet weekend, face like the back end of a bus . . .

Fred Karno's army

Archaic accusation of incompetence. Fred Karno was a popular music hall (vaudeville) comic and, presumably, not a noted military strategist. The insult refers to any organization marred by poor leadership, shoddy workmanship, or stifling bureaucracy.

Frog

French person

Funny peculiar

Way of describing a person or situation that is more odd and unsettling than amusing

"Funny he never married." "Funny peculiar."

Gannet

Greedy person

"You've only eaten all the egg and chips, you gannet!"

Git

Annoying person

Gobshite

A person regarded as mean and contemptible. From **gob**.

"That gobshite gobbed right into that other geezer's gob."

Go spare

Go berserk, to lose one's temper

"All I did was dent his car a little bit and he went spare!"

Gonk

Idiot; also a small troll-like stuffed toy that had grown to such popularity with British prepubescents in the mid-sixties that the Gonk craze was exploited with the hastily assembled movie *Gonks Go*

Beat, which included performances by such subsequently credible musicians as Ginger Baker and John McLaughlin

Gormless
Stupid, brainless

Happy as a sandboy
Outstanding example of eighteenth-century irony. Sandboys were employed to shovel sand up from pits, collect it, and peddle it to pub landlords and butchers for the purposes of spreading it around the floors of their establishments. It was arduous and underpaid work. There may have been some sandboys blessed with an optimistic outlook but most of them were so down in the mouth that the phrase "happy as a sandboy" was sardonically coined in their honor. It probably didn't make them particularly happy.

Hard lines
Tough luck

He thinks he's it
Someone with a high opinion of himself

Herbert
A foolish or dull person

His Nibs
Term of affection or derision, applied to a self-important person whether a boss, a husband, or a parent

Hoity toity
One who puts on airs

"I wouldn't touch him with a bargepole"
"I wouldn't touch him with a ten-foot pole"

"I've seen more life in a tramp's vest"
Insult implying that the target is a shiftless, lifeless, unmotivated slacker who has less get-up-and-go than the diseases and insects squirming around on the inside of a homeless person's undershirt

Jobsworth
Phrase used mainly in the music business to derisively describe someone—usually a janitor, doorman, or security guard—who adheres strictly to the rules of his or her job, no matter how trivial, for fear that the breaking of even the most minor rule will result in being fired (derived from the phrase "it's more than my job's worth")

Keep your hair on
Calm down (the more receding you are, the more insulting it becomes)

Knobhead
Dickhead

Lady Muck
Woman who thinks she's all that, even though her personal circumstances are no different than those around her (also **common as muck**: reaction of others to woman who thinks she's all that)

Lairy
Loud

"He's a right lairy sod."

Left footer
Catholic; derived from a notion commonly held in Northern Ireland that Catholic farmworkers used their left foot to push their shovels and Protestants their right

Ligger
Freeloader; used most frequently in the music business to describe someone whose raison d'être is to get his name on guest lists, worm his way backstage, and abscond with as many free gifts and goodie bags as is humanly possible

Looking like a lemon
Looking like a fool

Luvvie
Derogatory term for a breed of posh, self-involved British actor prone to gushing about craft and his or her wonderful, delightful colleagues in a possibly sincere but toe-curlingly patronizing manner. Kenneth Branagh and Emma Thompson in their married heyday were considered the epitome of luvviness. Ironically, the more they attempted to appear down-to-earth and unaffected, the more luvvie-

like they seemed. The *Harry Potter* movies are the Luvvie Woodstock.

Manky
Dirty

Mean
Tight-fisted, stingy

Mentalist
Crazy person; made famous by Steve Coogan's sitcom character Alan Partridge when he escaped the clutches of a scarily devoted fan screaming, "You're a mentalist!"

Minger
Unattractive female; also **boiler, slapper, munter**

Muppet
Foolish person

Not batting on a full wicket
Eccentric, mentally subnormal

Oik
Working-class person

"Step away from one's lawn or I'll set the dogs on you, you grubby little oik."

On your bike
A curt dismissal

Pants
Something that is of poor quality

"These new pants are pants!"

Pikey
Insulting term for a gypsy; a corruption of "turnpike"

Pillock
Fool or idiot

Plonker
Foolish person (another word that passed into the national lexicon due to exposure on the BBC sitcom *Only Fools and Horses*)

Poof
Homosexual male

Prannet
Idiot

Prat
A dismissive rather than malicious term for a foolish or incompetent person

Push the boat out
Celebrate

Rough as a badger's arse
Unsophisticated person

Round the twist
Crazy, insane

Scruff
Unkempt or dirty person

Slaphead
Balding person

Sling your hook
Boisterous command to an offending person to remove himself from the immediate vicinity; derived from naval slang.

If the state of a sailor's hammock failed to pass morning inspection, the phrase "Sling your hook" was bawled at him.

So-and-so
An unreliable person of poor character

"I'd like to give that so-and-so what for."

Soft in the head
Simple, backward

Sonny Jim
Condescending way of addressing someone, usually a younger person who needs to be put firmly in his place by an older, more experienced authority figure

"Don't come into my manor and tell me what's what, Sonny Jim."

Soppy
Week, feeble

Spanner
Idiot. U.S. equivalent: tool.

Specky four eyes
Juvenile reference to a person wearing glasses

Spoonerism
The transposition of the first letters of two words to hilarious effect, for example, cunning stunt, shining wit, sick duck, etc. Attributed to Anglican clergyman Rev. William Archibald Spooner from whose mouth a wealth of such gaffes accidentally stumbled. The humorous practice was kept alive and popularized by British comic Ronnie Barker whose 1970s sketch show *The Two Ronnies* probably didn't include a spoonerism skit every week—*it only seemed that way.*

Sunshine
An informal address that might seem on the surface to be a friendly and affectionate way of referring to a close companion but which carries a threatening subtext. A man who addresses another as "sunshine" is frequently out to intimidate and establish dominance.

"That's a nice little car you've got there, sunshine. What does it run on, prayer?"

Talk out of one's arse
Talk nonsense

Thicko
Dimwit

Toe rag
An obnoxious, worthless, sniveling, untrustworthy person

Toffee nosed
Snobbish, stuck up (also **toff**)

Trainspotter
A person, usually male, obsessed with trivia, facts, collecting, observing, and making notes. Term began as a description of rail enthusasists who hung around the nation's train stations noting the arrival and departure times of trains, and has evolved into a derogatory term for someone whose obsessive interests take the place of having a life, you know, like someone who complies comprehensive lists of British slang. For example. (See also **anorak**.)

Twit
Idiot

Up a gum tree

Confused, unable to come up with a solution to an outstanding problem

Wally

Idiot, buffoon, amiable loser

Wet

Feeble or weak person

"Don't be so wet. It's only a dead cat, you can buy another one."

Windbag

Pompous person who loves to drone on and on

Window licker

Mentally retarded person, celebrated in song by Aphex Twin

Woofter

Homosexual

The Army
Get Some In!

Ack Ack
Term used to describe antiaircraft fire (also, **Flak**)

Bombardier
Royal artillery corporal

Bully beef
Canned corn beef that was the main source of nourishment for the British troops

Civvy Street
The return to civilian life after a term of military service

Conscription
The draft

Dud
A shell that failed to explode

Ex–Service man
Veteran

Get some in
Put in some time; get some experience under your belt

Glasshouse
Military prison or detention center

Gong
Military medal

Mufti
Old army expression meaning civilian clothes

Old sweat
Term used to describe an experienced soldier

Remembrance Day
Veterans' Day

Sapper
Private in the Royal Engineers

Tommy
World War I slang for British soldier; short for Thomas Atkins

The Bathroom
Off for a Tom Tit

A slash
The act of urination

"I'm just off for a slash."

The bog
The toilet

Convenience
Painfully polite euphemism for restroom

"If it's not too much trouble could I use your convenience?"

Khazi
The toilet

Lav
Toilet (also **loo**)

Let off
Fart

Spend a penny
Go to the bathroom

Waz
Urinate, as in "I'm just off for a waz."

The Locals
The Neighbors

Bog-trotter
Derogatory term for someone of
Irish parentage

Brummie
Native of Birmingham

Geordie
A native of Newcastle; also the
name of the singsong dialect he
speaks

Jock
Catchall term for Scotsmen

Manc
A person from the Manchester
area

Mancunian
Native of Manchester (also
Manc)

Paddy
Catchall term for Irishmen

Sassenach
Derisive Scots term for the
English

Scally
Short for "scallywag," young
working-class Liverpudlian who
tends to be clad in trendy
sportswear

Schemie

Someone who comes from a Scottish council estate, known as a scheme

Soap dodger

Smelly, dirty person; Edinburgh term for Glaswegians

Taffy

Welsh person (also known as **Taff**)

Moaning Minnies
Classic British Expressions of Disappointment, Irritation, and Suspicion

All over the shop
Someone or something that is in a disheveled or disorganized state of affairs

"He was all over the shop when I bumped into him, couldn't make out a blooming word he was saying!"

At it
Up to no good

Brassed off
Fed up, annoyed

Browned off
Ticked off, annoyed by someone's thoughtless behavior

Can't be arsed
Can't be bothered

"Chance would be a fine thing"
Perfect distillation of British pessimism and the enthusiasm at crushing the dreams of others. The slightest exhibition of aspiration or ambition "What I really want to do is quit this soul-destroying nine to five and start my own fancy tea-kettle business" is inevitably followed by a dispirited, surrendering "Chance would be a fine thing." Also wielded as a weapon by disapproving family members, scornful and slightly intimidated by the notion that one of their own might elevate herself above her surroundings.

"I'm going to do it. I'm going to start that kettle business!" "Chance would be a fine thing!"

Cheesed off
Annoyed; mildly depressed

Clapped out
Worn out, no longer functioning

"The telly's clapped out just like everything else in this clapped-out clapper of a clap-trap house."

Cobblers
Rubbish

"That's a load of old cobblers!"

Cock-up
A mistake

"Made a bit of a cock-up there, haven't we?"

Dear
Expensive

Dog's breakfast
A mess (also dog's dinner)

"You might want to go and stay at a hotel for the next few weeks. I've made a bit of a dog's breakfast out of repairing the roof."

Faff around
Waste time

Hacked off
Annoyed (also **miffed** and **narked**)

It's all gone tits up
It's all gone horribly wrong (also known as **It's all gone Pete Tong**)

Jack in
Give up or stop doing something

"My job is boring, I'm going to jack it in."

Jack-the-lad
Confident, cocky, untrustworthy young man

Jerry-built
Poorly constructed

Made a fist of things
Screwed things up

Make a total bollocks of
Screw it up

Moaning Minnie
Constant complainer

Muck up
Spoil or ruin something

Mug
A gullible, foolish person, easily taken advantage of

Muggins
Passive-aggressive reference to oneself as being taken advantage of by all and sundry

"You go and enjoy yourself, muggins here will do all the work."

"Not in the same street"
Belittling comparison

"Blackpool's fine for the weekend but it's not in the same street as Great Yarmouth."

Not much cop
Poor quality

On your uppers
In dire straits, experiencing hard times

"Look at you with your arse hanging out your trousers, you're on your uppers, ain't you mum?"

Pig's ear
A mess

"You've made a pig's ear of that."

Playing silly buggers
Acting the fool

Poxy
Unpleasant (also **grotty**)

Pull your finger out
Get a move on

Quite/Absolutely
In the UK, often an expression of slight disdain or at best a damning with faint praise. Brits, fancying themselves the global masters of faint priase and mild enthusiasm,

often find themselves taken aback when they hear overexcitable Americans describing something as "quite good" or "quite funny." All too soon they discover the Yanks aren't being stingy with praise, rather the U.S. "quite" is an expression of huge admiration.

Ropey
Of poor quality

Sick to the back teeth
Fed up

Sweet F. A.
Nothing; more acceptable abbreviation of sweet fuck-all, which itself is a more vulgar version of sweet Fanny Adams

Turn it up
A request that a voluble, annoying person conduct himself in a more modest manner

"Turn it up, mate, you're giving us GBH of the earhole here!"

Up a gumtree
In great difficulties

"You're up a gum tree there, mate. I don't know how you're going to get your toe out of that hole."

Money
Minted!

Ackers
Money

Current account
Checking account

Dosh
Money

Kitty
Collection of money put away every week by a group of friends or colleagues to be spent on a common cause.

Lolly
Money

Lovely jubbly
The most money obtained through the least amount of work, usually through the selling of stolen or low-quality goods (made popular on the long-running sitcom *Only Fools and Horses*, which followed a family of lovable Cockney rogues attempting to get rich through foolish schemes that inevitably went comically awry)

Minted
Rich

Monkey
Bookmakers' slang for 500 pounds

Pony
Bookmakers' slang for 25 pounds

Quids in
Rich

Readies
Money

Shell out
Pay for something

Skint
Having no money

Spondulicks
Money

Strapped
Bereft of something, usually money

"Give us a quid, mister, I'm strapped for cash."

Stump up
Pay what you owe; hand the money over

Wedge
Large amount of money

"Where's that wedge you owe me for handling that bit of business with the greyhound?"

Wonga
Money (Gypsy expression)

Music
Bleedin' Orrible Racket

Why is it that the British public seems to have embraced and discarded a bewilderingly diverse range of upheavals in popular music since the 1960s? Could it be that tastes change in the blink of an eye because people are ravenous for constant stimulation? Could it be that this small island is such a hotbed of creativity that new movements in music constantly overwhelm and supersede their predecessors? Or could it be that, from the '60s up until the end of the '80s, there were as many as four weekly music newspapers, all of whom justified their existence by conjuring up new trends on a weekly basis? I just don't know. But I do know that the following list makes reference to some musical trends of absolutely no importance and some that still reverberate to this day.

Anorak

Twee, jangly guitar pop performed by fey young men with floppy hair dressed in rain jackets known as anoraks. Thorough research reveals the etymology of this term can be traced back to me. At the start of the 1980s, I shared an apartment with a guy in one of these fey, jangly outfits. As the overgrown toddlers in his band would show up to practice, I would greet them with an affectionate "Still playing that anorak music of yours?" The term spread like avian flu but the original source was never attributed. Until now.

Grebo

Collective term for grubby, dreadlocked British bands from the mid-1990s who combined alternative rock and electronic dance music to produce a muddy, tuneless racket. Prime Grebo suspects include Ned's Atomic Dustbin, the Wonder Stuff, Pop Will Eat Itself, and the Levellers, the latter beloved by the un-washed new age hippie traveling folk who labeled themselves Crusties.

Northern Soul

A Bizarro World established in a bunch of clubs across the north of England in which teenagers consumed vast amounts of amphetamines and spent entire sleep-free weekends doing somersaults and spinning on their heads to flop Motown records and obscure regional American R&B rarities from the 1960s. Not only did Northern Soul aficionados pay obscene amounts for pristine copies of these rarities but, in the early '70s, there was such a heavily populated and dedicated constituency that several records so obscure that even the artists responsible for them had long forgotten their existence were propelled out of extinction and into the UK Top 40.

NWOBHM (or, the New Wave of British Heavy Metal, to give the movement its full title)

An umbrella term for British rock bands that favored punk's lack of pretensions, didn't want to play arenas or dress like Vikings, but still yearned to crank out twenty-minute guitar solos. NWOBHM's best-known exponents were, and still are, Def Leppard and Iron Maiden.

Oi!

Skinheads aggrieved and embittered by what they per-ceived as a betrayal of punk's working-class roots by art school dilettantes like the Clash started to form bands with the sworn intention of never straying beyond shouty three-chord declarations of ineptitude and belligerence. Leading lights of Oi! such as the Cockney Rejects, Blitz, and the 4-Skins immedi-ately attracted a rabid following. Unfortunately, that following was approximately 98 percent

Oi! 1980s
© Gavin Watson/PYMCA

Nazi. Even though Oi! went quickly down in flames, banned from the airwaves, unbookable in live venues, its members consigned to a life of interviews where they attempted to justify themselves along the lines of "I'm not a Nazi, I'm a patriot," it lives on as an influence among nondiscriminating American punks.

Pathetique

Unexpected offshoot of Oi! Accused of harboring fascist sympathizers amid their ranks, several Oi! practitioners changed direction and morphed into shouty, three-chord comedy bands. Bands with names like Splodgenessabounds, Peter and the Test Tube Babies, and the Toy Dolls were lumped under

the term Pathetic Punk, which rapidly mutated into the lovely Pathetique. Not only did these Pathetique groups succeed in quashing the Sieg Heiling element of their audience but they enjoyed brief chart careers.

Romo

Last gasp of the weekly music press. The period between the heyday of British punk (1977) and the rise of Acid House (1989) was filled with insta-trends invented by desperate hacks with a deadline to meet. Romo was the last recorded instance of such a trend emerging fully formed from the fevered imaginations of rock critics and taking on a life of its own. Romo was created in 1996 by some scribblers at the soon-to-be-defunct weekly *Melody Maker,* which came up with the notion that the London music scene was ablaze with bands slathered in makeup and frilly shirts, noodling away on synthesizers just like the New Romantic fops of the '80s. The imaginary trend not only inspired a few dissolute clubbers to form bands but also convinced a number of gullible record company lackeys to sign them up. When the first Romo record—by a group called Orlando, I believe—appeared on the racks, the joke was over and the trend immediately expired.

Skiffle

American blues played with more enthusiasm than efficiency on washboards, tea chests, tin trays, spoons, and cardboard boxes. The most internationally renowned skiffle performer was Lonnie Donegan, best known in America for the lovely and timeless "Does Your Chewing Gum Lose Its Flavor on the Bedpost Overnight."

Trad

Dixieland jazz played with more enthusiasm than proficiency; in the late 1950s and early '60s, trad rivaled rock 'n' roll for the affections of British record buyers, many of whom, especially the male demographic, regarded it as more authentic. The most internationally renowned trad performer was Acker Bilk, best known in America for the lovely and timeless "Stranger on the Shore."

2 Step Garage

The UK's furious sense of inferiority over not having produced or being able to credibly perform hip hop leads to the constant hailing of urban mini-trends as Britain's definitive answer to rap. The fast-paced syncopated club music known as 2 Step Garage came closest, throwing up, in singer Craig David, a performer charismatic enough to enjoy brief American success. 2 Step mutated into the far rougher Grime about which I'm a little bit too decrepit to possess any kind of useful opinion, except to say that it sounds like an angry chef in a crowded kitchen yelling orders at his flustered staff.

Planes, Trains & Automobiles

Belisha beacon
A Belisha beacon is a tall black-and-white pole topped by a flashing orange globe. They appear on either side of the road at zebra crossings in the United Kingdom. A few Belisha beacons are also to be seen in the former British colony of Hong Kong. They are named after Lewslie Hore-Belisha (1895–1957), the minister of transport who introduced them in 1934.

Bonnet of car
Hood of car

Boot of car
Trunk of car

"Can I give you a lift somewhere?"
"Can I give you a ride somewhere?"

Car park
Parking lot

Crash barrier
Guard rail

Diversion
Detour

Filling station
Gas station

Flyover
Overpass

Glove box
Glove compartment

Hooter
Car horn

Lorry
Truck

Mileometer
Odometer

Moped
Small motorbike, entirely lacking in power and the ability to imbue the rider with rough sexual charisma. Trust me. Though the moped has made inroads in the United States, its ubiquity and inability to inspire awe have not yet thoroughly infected the youth of the nation.

Motor racing
Auto racing (or more commonly, just NASCAR)

Motorway
Highway, freeway

Number plate
License plate or tag

Petrol
Gasoline

Railway carriage
Passenger car on a train

Return ticket
Round-trip ticket

Ring Road
A circular route around a town. Compare U.S. equivalent: bypass.

Windscreen
Windshield

Wing (of a car)
Fender

Zebra crossing
Striped pedestrian crossing. U.S. equivalent is crosswalk.

Politics
Order! Order!

Back benches

The seats reserved in the Houses of Parliament for politicians who are neither ministers nor spokesmen for their parties. The backbencher fills the vital function of booing loudly and coughing derisively into his or her hands when members of the opposition attempt to speak. Backbenchers in the House of Lords have the added responsibility of snoring loudly.

Beefeaters

Or the Yeomen of the Guard, to give them their full title. Their job is to search the cellars of Westminster in case any aggrieved renegade has attempted to re-create Guy Fawkes's Gunpowder Plot. Other than that, their duties are entirely ceremonial.

Black Rod

Or the Gentleman Usher of the Black Rod, to give him his full title. Black Rod's day-to-day function is seeing that the denizens of the House of Lords have comfy cushions to sit on. But he is best known to the public for the role he plays in the ceremonial State Opening of Parliament when he bangs on the door of the House of Commons with a big black rod to summon the MP's to the House of Lords to hear the queen's speech.

By-election

When an MP dies, becomes eligible for the House of Lords, or is forced, by tabloid revelation of a sex scandal, to resign, his seat in the Commons becomes vacant and a by-election is arranged to fill his place.

Chancellor of the Exchequer

Head of the Treasury, who prepares the budget

Crossing the Floor

Changing political allegiance. Members of opposing parties sit on opposite sides of the House of Commons. An MP who feels that he can no longer in good faith be seen to support the lies, corruption, and moral decay for which his party has come to be synonymous registers his epiphany by crossing the floor to take up position with the other party, whose morals are obviously above reproach. The most famous example of crossing the floor is Winston Churchill who, in 1904, left the Conservative party and joined the Liberal party, with whom he remained until recrossing the floor and officially rejoining the Tories in 1925, thus enabling him to come up with the deathless quote, "Any man who is under thirty and is not a liberal has no heart and any man who is over thirty and is not a conservative has no brains."

Devolution

Decentralization of government power, which has led, in recent years, to the establishment of the Scottish Parliament, the National Assembly for Wales, and the Northern Ireland Assembly

Lib Dems

Liberal Democrat party; formed in 1988 from the ashes of the Social Democratic party and the Liberal party, in order to elevate members from the status of powerless third party into a coalition able to effect social change and give the British people an alternative to the two-party system. To date, it has remained a powerless third party with no power to effect social change.

Mace

Another example of the ceremony and tradition that characterizes the British political process. The mace is a staff of office that stands as a symbol of the power and authority vested on the House of Commons by the monarchy. At the start and close of every day, the mace is carried in and out of the chamber of the Commons. Then and only then, the arguing, threats, and slander can begin.

Naming of a Member

If a politician behaves in a consistently disreputable fashion he or she is disciplined by being named. During debates, MPs address each other by the laborious title "The Right Honorable Member for . . ." But if their behavior is too disgraceful to countenance, the Speaker addresses them by their actual given name. You might not consider that much of a punishment but, let me tell you, Richard Tinycock and Heywood Jablowme have been the models of propriety ever since.

"Order! Order!"

The beleaguered prime minister, forced to support an archaic and unpopular bill in order to maintain the loyalty of mutinous cabinet members, stands up and delivers the speech of his life, reminding everyone who'd lost faith in him of his old fire and quashing any notion of rebellion in the would-be traitors. The House erupts. The bewhiskered old Speaker attempts to calm the cacophony, calling out "Order! Order!"

Serjeant at arms

The House of Commons equivalent of Black Rod; employed to ensure the order and security of the House. Most important, the serjeant at arms is the only person in the Commons allowed to carry a sword. There's a martial-arts fish-out-of-water movie just dying to be made out of that: "Parliamentary Samurai"!

Tory

Member of the Conservative party

Woolsack

A large square cushion made of wool and covered in red cloth. The Lord Chancellor in the House of Lords sits on it.

Posh

Boater
Hard, flat-topped straw hat sported by upper-class twits who enjoy punting on the river

The Chattering Classes
Columnists, broadcasters, and journalists who greatly value their own opinions on current affairs. Used as a pejorative term by conservative commentators who regard them as windbag liberals who make a living discussing and bemoaning the problems that beset contemporary society without participating in any move to effect change.

Chinless wonder
Derisory term for an upper-class male

Come up
Arrive as a student at Oxford or Cambridge

Dame
A lady who has been knighted

"Dame Judi Dench was simply luminous in The Chronicles of Riddick.*"*

Debag
Forcibly remove someone's trousers as a frightfully amusing prank

Don
College tutor; derived from the Latin *dominus,* meaning master, lord, owner, or host

Double-barreled
Two-pronged surname joined by a hyphen, for example, Smithers-Jones, Baden-Powell, Bonham-Carter

Hooray Henry
Braying, empty-headed, unemployable, champagne-guzzling male member of the upper classes

Jolly hockey sticks
Dismissive description of the athletic inclination of British public school girls where hockey is more important than academic progress

Punt
Flat-bottomed boat steered—or punted—with a pole

Rag Week
College ritual where posh students go on a rampage of destruction, abduction, and debagging in the name of charity

Sent down
When a student at Oxford or Cambridge behaves so abominably that even the influence and checkbook of their parents can't persuade the authorities to turn a blind eye, the miscreant is expelled or "sent down," thus preparing them for a career in government.

Sloane Ranger
Affectionately pejorative term for privileged, conservative, public school–educated, horse-riding upper-middle-class young woman who lives and/or socializes in the vicinity of London's Sloane Square. Princess Diana is the patron saint of Sloanes.

Toffee nosed
Stuck up, snobbish, hoity-toity, one who looks down on others as social inferiors

Upper-class twit
Derogatory term referring to members of the ruling social hierarchy, specifically the male specimens whose braying enunciation was so deftly portrayed in Monty Python's "Upper-Class Twit of the Year" sketch

Work
The Professionals

Barrister
Trial lawyer

Cashier
Bank teller

Char
Cleaning woman, maid

Chemist
Pharmacist

Clippie
Female fare collector on bus service

Cloakroom attendant
Coat check person

Commercial traveler
Traveling salesman

Dispatch rider
Messenger

Dustman
Garbage collector

Estate agent
Realtor

Fishmonger
Fish seller

Fruit dealer
Fruit seller

Gaffer
Foreman, boss

Greengrocer
Seller of fruit and vegetables

Haberdasher
Seller of dressmaking accessories

Hairdresser
Barber

Ironmonger
Term for both the hardware store
and the proprietor of same

Joiner
Carpenter

Lollipop man
Crossing guard

Matron
Head nurse

Minder
Bodyguard, personal security

Newsreader
Newscaster

Solicitor
Attorney

Spark
Electrician

Totter
Rag and bone man; UK equivalent of the junk man

A bit on the side
Infidelity

A good seeing to
Sexual intercourse

Bash the bishop
Late-nineteenth-century euphemism for masturbation derived,
some say, from the resemblance between the penis and a chess bishop

Bazonkers
Breasts

Cottaging
Once on the margins, now
mainstream thanks to George
Michael, cottaging is the practice

Bill Clinton had a bit on the side
Credit: Peter Casolino/Alamy

of cruising public toilets in search
of an amenable stranger for
purposes of anonymous sex.
Much nicer name, though. Makes

you think of thatched roofs and roaring fires and scones with clotted cream. Well, that's what it makes me think of, anyway.

Crumpet

Female object of 1970s desire. The '70s UK libido was stimulated by Bond girls, the bouncy blond barmaids populating the *Carry On* movies, the lesbian vampires from the Hammer horror films, the shrieking blondes fleeing from Benny Hill, the unclad girls next door who decorated Page 3 of the *Sun,* and the double entendre–spouting stars of sitcoms like *Are You Being Served.* All of them fell under the appreciative classification "crumpet." The most notorious example of crumpet crossing the Atlantic to receive a rapturous American reception was Samantha Fox.

Dogging

Voyeuristic pastime involving couples lurking in parking garages watching other couples having sex in their vehicles. The practice gained its own George Michael–like hero after reporters from the *Sun* exposed former Liverpool soccer star Stan Collymore as a habitual dogger. British car-parking garages are now potential mine-fields of embarrassment and humiliation as neophytes unversed in dogging etiquette will approach couples with no interest in being watched while they fumble for their keys.

Fancy the pants off

Sexually desire someone so intensely that their clothes spontaneously disappear. Only the first four words of the previous sentence are technically accurate.

Fanny magnet

Something or somebody who exudes sexual magnetism no woman can resist

"Jim's collection of rare books makes him a fanny magnet."

More realistic example:

"Jim's Ferrari, his Beverly Hills mansion, and unlimited credit make him a fanny magnet."

Actually neither is true.

Fit

Sexually attractive

French letter

Condom

Gagging for it

Excitement at the prospect of a forthcoming event, usually a sexual encounter. The villain in *Mission Impossible 2* perplexed international audiences when he announced that he was gagging for it just before employing a cigar cutter to slice off the finger of an underling foolish enough to suggest that the object of the bad guy's thwarted desire wasn't, in fact, gagging for it.

Get your leg over

Have sexual intercourse

"Get your tits out for the lads!"

Nonironic exhortation aimed by a gathering of intoxicated males to a lone female, generally sung to the melody of "My Darling Clementine." Soccer matches and public houses tend to inspire spontaneous outbursts.

Give her/him one

Have sex with

Half mast

(1) Your zipper is halfway down.
(2) Your erection is not fully realized.

Knee trembler

Hurried sex in a standing position

Knocking shop

Brothel

Minge

Vagina (also **fanny**)

On the game

Involved in prostitution

On the pull

Looking for a sexual partner

"Phwoar"

Vocal exclamation of appreciation expressed toward object of desire. Used as a semi-ironic rallying cry with the mid-nineties advent of UK lads' magazines spearheaded by *Loaded*.

Rumpy-pumpy

Sexual intercourse

Slap and tickle

Lighthearted term for sexual intercourse

Slip her a length
Have sex with a willing female

Snog
Make out with someone

Stunna
Tabloid term for attractive unclad female

Tipping the velvet
Victorian euphemism for cunnilingus; best known as the title of Sarah Waters's saucy lesbians-in-love novel and the BBC miniseries starring the frequently employed Keeley Hawes

Top shag
The person you really want to be shagging. As opposed to the person you actually are shagging. Who is thinking fondly of the person they'd rather be shagging while you're shagging them. Ah, the circle of life.

Totty
Sexually attractive female; modern equivalent of crumpet

Wank
Masturbate

Wankbank
The reliable mental repertory company who accompany a tragic night of solitary loveless self-entertainment

Wanking chariot
Bed

Would
Abbreviated declaration of male desire. There are varying forms of "would," each of which expresses a slightly different way of saying substantially the same thing.

"I would": I would have sex with that woman under any circumstances.

"You would": No matter how much you protest or try to put up a front of indifference, it is obvious that you would have sex with that woman under any circumstances.

"I still would": I have learned a lot about that woman, her character, her morals, and her background, and it has all shocked me. Nothing can be gained by associating with her for a minute more yet I would have sex with that woman under any circumstances.

"You still would": You are desperate.

"Would you?": Underhand method of gauging exactly how low someone's standards are.

Your hole
Sex

"Did you get your hole last night or were you too paralytic?"

Shop
Shopping

Carrier bag
Shopping bag

Cheap at half the price
Street trader's cry, meaning the item for sale is less expensive than if it was sold at full price, lives on in an ironic sense; if sellers use this phrase they're telling you to your face that they're about to con you and you will end up paying for substandard goods or services.

"Buy this book, cheap at half the price."

The Chinky
Racist, but affectionate, term for the Chinese restaurant from which Brits purchase take-out food

Flog
Sell something.

The Paki
Racist, but affectionate, term for the Pakistani corner shop from which Brits purchase newspapers, soft drinks, cigarettes, and lottery tickets

Precinct
Shopping area, strip mall

Punnet of strawberries
Box of strawberries

Sports
"I'm a Bit of a Rugger Bugger!"

Arrows
Darts

The Beautiful Game
Reverent phrase used by the emotionally retarded to describe soccer

Blinder
Spectacular performance on the soccer field by a player or a team

"The lad played a blinder!"

Blocker
A batsman in cricket who plays too defensively

Chinaman
In cricketing parlance, a ball bowled by a left-arm wrist spinner, which spins into a right-handed batsman. Which is bad. Or good.

Conkers
Chestnuts hardened in vinegar put on strings used by schoolchil-

The beautiful game
© Jon Ingledew/PYMCA

dren in battles where the aim is to destroy a rival with the force with which you aim your own (it's also fun if you strike your opponent's fingers)

Dribbling

Mystical footwork by which a soccer player jogs with the ball in a leisurely fashion and then breaks into a sudden spurt, propelling the ball past his stunned opponent, leaving him dribbling with frustration

Googly

Another cricket term: a ball bowled by a wrist spinner that turns the opposite way

Goose step

This means a change in running style from a sprint to a high kicking in order to slow down a defender, only to sprint once the defender has slowed down. Apparently first used by a player trying to avoid stomping through a pile of dogshit that lay in his path.

Grubber

In the world of British rugby, this means a mistimed dropkick from anywhere in the field.

Hat-trick

Cricket term for taking three wickets by three successive balls. Even among those for whom the word "cricket" induces instant catatonia, the term has become synonymous with anything that happens in threes and has translated well to the sport of ice hockey.

Hooker

Rugby term referring to the front-row player in a scrum whose function is to try and hook the ball. What he does on his own time is, of course, none of our business.

"It's a game of two halves"

One of the great defining clichés from the UK soccer commentator's arsenal of the obvious.

Maul

Rugby talk: free-for-all brawl

Pitch

Sports field

Plank

Poorly performing cricket bat, i.e., one that vibrates in the batsman's hands. A bad workman always blames his tools.

Slogger

More cricket: a batsman who hits the ball across the line

Sticky wicket

Cricketing term describing a method of bowling so super-natural it seems to change direction before it reaches the befuddled batsman. The term has come to be synonymous with a complicated situation.

Strip

What soccer players wear (also known as **kit**)

Studs

Cleats

Tackle

Steal the ball

Bizarre Pronunciations
Ioan Gruffudd?

The discrepancy between the way a name—be it of a person or a district—is written and the sometimes very different pronunciation can lead to unbridled condescension and icy stares. Before attempting to ask directions to a locale with a tricky name or inquire after the welfare of a Brit with a colorful surname, memorize this brief guide.

Beauchamp
Beecham

Cholmondeley
Posh surname, looks like it's going to be a mouthful but turns out to be the simple "Chumley"

Cockburn
This one's a potential minefield of embarrassment and mocking corrections; unless you're of a superior social status and feel comfortable humiliating a guest by mispronouncing his surname, the correct way to say it is "Coburn."

Culzean
Ah, Culzean Castle. Many's the happy hour I've spent in this picturesque Scottish castle hotel. Why was I so happy? Because of the breathtaking view of the Isle of Arran? Or because I knew enough to pronounce the name, which is, of course, "Culain."

Dalziel

You're watching TV with aged British relatives. The long-running cop show *Dalziel and Pascoe* comes on. Your most advisable course of action is to plead diarrhea and lock yourself in the bathroom. If etiquette forbids you making a speedy exit and you're forced to endure the sedate drama, on no account refer to the first name of the disparate titular partnership as "Dalzeel." It is properly pronounced "Dee-el."

Magdalen College

Your stay at this prestigious Oxford seat of learning will be less traumatic if you learn to use the proper pronunciation: "Maudlin."

Mainwaring

Unless you're a fan of being spoken to with the kind tones reserved for the mentally challenged, always pronounce this surname "Mannering."

Menzies

Scottish surname pronounced "Mingis," on no account to be confused with **minger**

Milngavie

Should you be tempted to visit this picturesque Scottish village on the outskirts of Glasgow renowned for the manufacturing of cardboard boxes and flexible plastic ducting, you would be advised to use the proper pronunciation: "Mul-guy"

Slough

The home of Wernham-Hogg, reads like it should be pronounced "Sluff"; correct pronunciation rhymes with "cow"

St. John

The intimidation potential when confronted with a Brit sporting a double-barreled surname is grisly enough, but what if the first barrel of that surname is St. John? I'm telling you right now, do anything in your power to prevent yourself saying that name as it appears in print. Instead, memorize the words "Honest Injun" and use it to remind you to say "Sinjun."

Strachan

Scottish surname, the cause of much confusion and trepidation as you're never sure whether the owner of the name is happy to pronounce it as it reads or is a stickler for the more traditional "Strawn"

Worcester

The perfect way to reduce a lively dinner table to awkward silence is to ask someone to pass the sauce and refer to the condiment phonetically rather than by its proper pronunciation, which is "wooster."

The Weather

Brolly
Umbrella

Bucketing
Raining very heavily

Close
Humid

It's pissing it down
Raining so relentlessly and creating such nationwide misery and depression that the description merits that extra "it"

Nippy
Chilly, cold. Compare U.S. comedian Chevy Chase in the motion picture *National Lampoon's Christmas Vacation:* "It's a bit *nipply* out."

Parky
Cold

"Close the door, it's parky out there!"

Peasouper
Very thick fog

Peasouper
Credit: Craig Brown/Alamy

Pelting
Raining extremely heavily

Raining stair rods
Raining heavily

Miscellany

Fag

In the British public school (i.e., private fee-paying) system, a fag is a younger pupil forced to run errands for and uncomplainingly accept abuse from older students with the justification that it is a time-honored tradition that the elder person had proudly endured. The U.S. equivalent might be the hazing rituals a pledge has to endure before being admitted to a fraternity, except that fagging has no grand reward beyond leaving its victims emotionally scarred and sexually confused. In that respect, it's much like being a prison bitch.

Holiday camps

The 1960s was the first time that the generation gap became evident in British society. In the eyes of the generation that came of age during the hardships of the 1930s, the children of the '60s were a pampered, self-indulgent, ungrateful shower. But while the beneficiaries of the swinging '60s didn't endure conscription, rationing, or air raids, they shared one trauma in common with their embittered elders. If you were born any time between the mid-1930s and the end of the 1960s, there was a better than good chance of you having to spend at least one summer in a holiday camp. Although camps offering accommodation, meals, and entertainment at a reasonable price had been available since the late nineteenth century, it wasn't until an entrepreneur called Billy Butlin opened a self-named complex in the seaside town of Skegness that the holiday camp really became part of the national social calendar. All across the country, parents seeking a brief respite from the daily grind that forced them to get up at a certain time, depart for work at a certain time, and return home at a certain time shed their routines and headed for Butlin's holiday camp. There, they slept in tiny, cold chalets until they were forced to get out of bed at an arranged time, were shepherded into a canteen where they ate their meals, and were expected to retire back to their rooms before midnight. In between mealtime and bedtime, campers were cheerfully dragooned into participating in fun and games like the Knobbly Knees contest and the Glamorous Granny pageant. Ensuring that no camper weaseled his or her way out of the hilarity, Butlin's camp commandants of fun, the Redcoats, strong-armed any potential backsliders into participation.

Butlin's proved such an immediate and enduring success that two rival camps, Pontin's and Warner's, entered the market. Amazingly enough, the market was huge enough to contain all three rivals. It remained huge until the '70s when the airlines dropped their prices sufficiently that foreign holidays became affordable. Even though Majorca, Marbella, and Ibiza are the vacation destinations of choice for most Brits, Butlin's still survives, albeit in a reduced capacity, and bone-idle fathers are still being turfed out of their comfy deckchairs by psychotically enthusiastic Redcoats and persuaded to display their knobbly knees to the rest of the camp.

Kitchen sink drama

Grim, forbidding black-and-white movies chronicling the crushed dreams of British working-class youths trapped in dead-end northern towns that offered them nothing but the chance to follow their fathers down the mines or their mothers into child-rearing. John Osborne's 1956 play *Look Back in Anger* unshackled British drama from its role as a mirror to the aspirations, triumphs, downfalls, and foibles of the upper and middle classes. Even though the British film industry didn't make it out of the '60s, it spent much of that decade coughing up a string of gritty sagas—*Saturday Night and Sunday Morning, Room at the Top, The Loneliness of the Long-Distance Runner* among them—that laid the groundwork for *Coronation Street* and *Eastenders,* the gritty, strife-packed domestic soap operas that have ruled the UK TV ratings for the past thirty years. Bit of a mixed blessing, then.

Milk float

Small electric vehicle for home milk delivery; rather than reduce the milkman to a figure of derision, this comical vehicle actually added to the post–WWII perception of him as a daytime Lothario, coolly preying on the unfulfilled housewives of the country while their weary husbands trudged through another dull day at the office. For backup material, I refer you to Benny Hill's 1971 number one single, "Ernie, the Fastest Milkman in the West," coinciden-tally the first 45 I ever owned.

Pantomime

Christmas musical based on a popular fairy tale. Most young Brits' first, and often last, experience of live theater is being dragged at an early age to see a version of *Aladdin* or *Peter Pan* or *Cinderella* or *Puss in Boots* featuring a currently popular male sitcom, soap, pop, or reality-TV star in drag spouting double entendres or a currently popular female sitcom, soap, pop, or reality-TV star playing the dashing male lead and professing eternal devotion to a blushing female love interest. Audience participation is para-mount in these productions, specifically when the villain of the piece sneaks up behind the unsuspecting drag lead and the excited audience members are entreated to scream, "He's behind you!" It would be easy to say that, over the centuries, the pure and innocent intentions behind the pantomime have been debased by commercial concerns and TV-bred vulgarity. This is not the case. Pantomimes have always been a vehicle for comics and singers to peddle their wares in front of insanely enthusiastic audiences. For British youth denied the benefits of a private school education, a visit at a young age to a pantomime instills almost the same amount of sexual confusion. But without the beatings.

Silly season

Tabloid parlance for the barren month of August when the UK Parliament is in recess, the majority of the D-list celebrities with whom they have a reciprocally exploitative arrangement are on vacation, but a daily paper still needs to be produced and crammed full of salacious content. Thus, August is filled with front-page stories about two-headed cats, outbreaks of sneezing, outbreaks of hand-wringing moralizing, and obsessive coverage of celebrities previously deemed too desperate to acknowledge. Except for August 2005 when Jude Law bonked the nanny.

Index

Index

Index

Index

Index

Index

Index

Index

Index